beginnings

longing to belong

Around the Fire
A Participant's Companion

Andy Langford, Mark Ralls,
and Rob Weber

Abingdon Press / Nashville

Beginnings: Longing to Belong
Around the Fire: A Participant's Companion

This book is printed on acid-free, elemental chlorine-free paper.

ISBN 978-0-687-65012-5

08 09 10 11 12 13 14 15 16 17 — 10 9 8 7 6 5 4 3 2 1

MANUFACTURED IN THE UNITED STATES OF AMERICA

Contents

Introduction

This book is a resource for participants and leaders in local congregations that are offering *Beginnings: Longing to Belong*. This resource is used in conjunction with *Beginnings: Video Resources,* a set of video presentations that begin the dialogue, and *Beginnings: Participant's Guide,* a workbook for program participants.

Welcome!

So those people in Jerusalem who welcomed Simon Peter's message about Jesus Christ were baptized, and on that day of Pentecost about three thousand persons became followers of Jesus Christ.

All of these followers of Jesus Christ devoted themselves to the first disciples' teaching and fellowship, the holy meal of bread and cup, and prayer. Everyone was filled with awe, and many wonders and miracles were accomplished.

All who believed lived in close fellowship and possessed all things in common. They sold their belongings and property and gave their money to anyone who had need. Day by day, the followers of Jesus Christ spent much time together in the temple in Jerusalem. They shared meals together from home to home. They ate their food with joy and thanksgiving, praising God and showing kindness to everyone. And day by day, the Lord God increased the number of persons who were being saved.

(Acts 2:41-47, authors' paraphrase)

What is the church? When many persons think of the word *church,* a building comes to mind. Some picture a soaring Gothic cathedral. Other folk see a white clapboard house of worship with a simple steeple. Some recall a storefront facility in a decaying downtown or an urban warehouse where young Christians gather to sing praise songs. Still other people picture an adobe hut in the American

Southwest or a house-church in Central America. However different our images, all of us share the notion that the church is a place where certain things happen—events such as worship and Bible study and fellowship meals. The church is also more than this, however. Church is not just a place on a map. A building is something some churches have, but it is not what a church really is.

People also see the church as an institution. Thumb through the "churches" section of your local Yellow Pages and you will find listed many different congregations representing many different kinds of organizations. You will see the Adventist Church, the Unitarian Universalist Church, and organizations whose names begin with every letter in between. These names represent different institutions with different commitments, structures, and networks. Yet, the church is more than just some kind of religious corporation. The institution is like the bark of a living tree. The bark gives structure but essentially is dead. The real life of each of these groups comes from the interaction of its participants.

Will Campbell, a Southern Baptist preacher, lives just outside Nashville, Tennessee. In addition to being a preacher, Campbell has also been a civil rights activist, a farmer, and an author of books for children and adults. In one of his books, Campbell gives a description of the church, voiced by a friend named P.D.

In Mississippi during the 1960s, a student who had been studying for the Christian ministry was killed following a civil rights protest. P.D., distressed with the response of Christians to the violence, said:

> "You know, Preacher Will, that church of yours and Mr. Jesus is like an Easter chicken [a tiny chick dyed a bright color and sold in the spring for children to own as pets] my little Karen got one time. Man, that chicken was a pretty thing. Dyed a deep purple. Bought it at the grocery store....
>
> "But pretty soon that baby chicken started feathering out. You know, sprouting little pin feathers. Wings and tail and all that. And you know what? Them new feathers weren't purple. No sirree bob, that ... chicken wasn't really purple at all. That chicken was a Rhode

> Island Red. And when all them little red feathers started growing out from under that purple it was ... a sight. All of a sudden Karen couldn't stand that chicken any more....
>
> "Well, we took that half-purple and half-red thing out to her Grandma's house and threw it in the chicken yard with all the other chickens.... And now you can't tell one chicken from another. They're all just alike. That Easter chicken is just one more chicken. There ain't a ... thing different about it."
>
> Preacher Will responded to his friend, "Well, P.D., the Easter chicken is still useful. It lays eggs doesn't it?"
>
> P.D. answered, "Yea, Preacher Will. It lays eggs.But they all lay eggs. Who needs an Easter chicken for that? And the Rotary Club serves coffee. And the 4-H Club says prayers. The Red Cross takes up offerings for hurricane victims. Mental Health does counseling, and the Boy Scouts have youth programs."[1]

How do Christians live their lives together? Is the church just like P.D.'s Easter chicken? Or is the church something else altogether? We believe that Christianity is a culture and a lifestyle lived in community with other persons who also follow Jesus Christ.

In this book we introduce what for some may be a new way of seeing the church but one that recalls ancient practices. We will suggest that church is living together in true community. Church gathers around the fire of the Holy Spirit and shares in the warmth of our life together. Being church is something we do—and do together—as a living expression of our commitment to Jesus Christ.

This understanding comes from observing the practices of the early church. The story of the first Christians is told in the fifth book of the New Testament, called The Acts of the Apostles. In twenty-eight short chapters, Acts covers the first thirty years of Christianity as it spread from Jerusalem across the Roman Empire. Here the church is described with the Greek word *koinonia*. This word is often translated as "fellowship," but it means more than we usually do when we use the word. *Koinonia* is intimate fellowship with God and God's people, the kind of fellowship that binds persons together in love and trust. *Koinonia* is more than just a group of people coming together because they like each other's company or believe similar things about God. *Koininia* exists as Christians share life together and experience the life-giving power of true community.

Unfortunately, we rarely experience such authentic community because of our tendency to prize individualism, independence, and self-sufficiency. Sadly, in our culture we view this pursuit of a solitary life as a sign of maturity. As a result, we grow up assuming that we should outgrow the very things that make life meaningful and vital: interdependence, sharing, and caring. In his book *All I Really Need to Know I Learned in Kindergarten,* Robert Fulghum describes how he discovered his healthiest vision of life at an early age when he attended his church's Sunday school:

> All I really need to know about how to live and what to do and how to be I learned in kindergarten, ... there in the sand-pile at Sunday school....
>
> Share everything.
> Play fair.
> Don't hit people....
> Say you're sorry when you hurt someone....
> Live a balanced life....
> When you go out into the world, watch out for traffic, hold hands, and stick together.
> Be aware of wonder. Remember the little seed in the Styrofoam cup: The roots go down and the plant goes up and nobody really knows how or why, but we are all like that. [2]

Life really is about interdependence, sharing, and caring. The early Christians learned this from one another when they were initiated into the new community of Jesus through baptism. They shared everything from financial resources to a holy meal they called Communion. They discovered how to resolve their conflicts with fairness and compassion. Together they folded their hands in worship and then extended them—both to one another and to strangers—in fellowship. Together they became more aware of the signs and wonders of God's presence among them. All of this made them into something more than a building or an organization. They became a living organism, with the deep roots of common memories and the vibrant growth of shared experiences.

The deep, rich, exciting *koinonia* of the early church is not to be left on the pages of history. We are invited to be church as well. Join us as we explore this new way of being in Jesus Christ.

---

1. From *Brother to a Dragonfly,* by Will Campbell (Seabury Press, 1977); pages 217–20.

2. From *All I Really Need to Know I Learned in Kindergarten,* by Robert Fulghum (Ballantine Books, 1986); pages 4–5.

One:
Longing to Belong?

Introduction

"The soul hardly ever realizes it, but ... loneliness is really a homesickness for God."

Hubert Van Zeller

SPIRITUAL HUNGER

In my former book [The Gospel According to Luke], Theophilus, I wrote about all that Jesus began to do and to teach until the day he was taken up to heaven, after giving instructions through the Holy Spirit to the apostles he had chosen. After his suffering, he presented himself to them and gave many convincing proofs that he was alive. He appeared to them over a period of forty days and spoke about the kingdom of God. On one occasion, while he was eating with them, he gave them this command: "Do not leave Jerusalem, but wait for the gift my Father promised, which you have heard me speak about. For John baptized with water, but in a few days you will be baptized with the Holy Spirit....

"You will receive power when the Holy Spirit comes on you; and you will be my witnesses in Jerusalem, and in all Judea and Samaria, and to the end of the earth." After he said this, he was taken up before their very eyes, and a cloud hid him from their sight....

When the day of Pentecost came, they were all together in one place. Suddenly a sound like the blowing of a violent wind came from heaven and filled the whole house where they were sitting.

They saw what seemed to be tongues of fire that separated and came to rest on each of them. All of them were filled with the Holy Spirit and began to speak in other tongues as the Spirit enabled them.

Now there were staying in Jerusalem God-fearing Jews from every nation under heaven. When they heard this sound, a crowd came together in bewilderment, because each one heard their own language being spoken....

When the people heard this, they were cut to the heart and said to Peter and the other apostles, "Brothers, what shall we do?" Peter replied, "Repent and be baptized."... Those who accepted his message were baptized, and about three thousand were added to their number that day.

(Acts 1:1-9; 2:1-41, excerpts)

HOMESICKNESS

Mark recalls:

When I was in my early thirties, I studied at a school in Germany for almost two years. I lived alone, and my research in the library was a solitary pursuit. I was sometimes lonely and often felt at least a twinge of homesickness. I found solace listening to a homeless street performer named Terry. Terry spent his days on the old stone bridge that I walked across on my way to the university. Every afternoon I would listen to Terry play American folk songs and would feel a nostalgic pull toward home.

Terry was a remarkable talent. Even though his voice sounded as if he had just gargled a handful of gravel, he knew how to work a crowd. He began with upbeat songs, singing with enthusiasm and grinning his toothless smile at everyone who passed by. Although he had not bathed in weeks, Terry was utterly charming. Crowds swelled around him. Young mothers forgot their caution, allowing shy children to drop coins furtively in his open guitar case while bolder ones danced around his feet.

With the skill of a consummate performer, Terry would gradually slow the pace of his repertoire and take us to a deeper, more introspective place. Terry always ended with his signature piece: Bob

> Dylan's classic, "Like a Rolling Stone." When this homeless man sang about living without roots or a place to call home, the crowd was stilled. It seemed irreverent to walk by or to toss money in his case. We knew instinctively that with this song, Terry was singing, not for us, but for himself.
>
> And yet, Terry was still singing about us. Homelessness is not just about where someone sleeps at night. Our homesickness is a condition of the soul—a dislocation of our hearts from the heart of God, a disconnection from the hearts of one another. Looking back, I now realize that I was not the only person on that bridge looking for a place to connect. In our own way, all of us were there searching for a home.

We find our home wherever we feel affirmed for who we really are and wherever we can learn to accept others with no strings attached. This means that what we call "home" is actually the experience of true community. Home is not just our childhood house or the town where we grew up. Home is more than just a place on a map. It is the assurance that we have a place in the heart of God and in the hearts of those people who love us.

When this kind of redemptive community is missing from our lives, we feel a nagging sense of loss, a deep longing to belong to something bigger than ourselves. In a Walker Percy novel, a character named Will Barrett is having a heated conversation with his psychologist, Dr. Scanlon:

> "Something is wrong, Scanlon."
> "What is it, Will?"
> "I'm homesick."
> "How long have you been homesick?"
> "All my life."[1]

WHERE EVERYBODY KNOWS YOUR NAME

Today, many of us feel like Will. We live in an increasingly mobile society where people are constantly pulling up roots, a fast-paced, demanding world where few find the time or energy to connect with each other. Generations ago, most people lived in close-knit neighborhoods where friends gathered on the front porch or at the town square to share the important events of their lives. Now the front porch has been replaced with the privacy of a back deck. The neighborhood has become a gated community. The town square has dissolved into suburbs of strangers. As a result, we are more likely to cocoon in our homes pursuing solitary activities: gaming on personal computers, listening to private play lists on our iPods, and ordering movies from our living room. These lifestyle changes have combined to turn us into isolated individuals, struggling to make it on our own.

Mark recalls:

> When I was in college, nobody went out or studied on Thursday night. We all gathered around the television to watch the most popular show of the decade. This show featured a group of misfits: an unemployed and overweight wisecracker, an insecure mailman, a middle-aged graduate student, a hardened single mom, and a washed-up baseball player. Somehow—almost miraculously—all these people who could not fit in anywhere else found a home in a Boston pub called Cheers. I think the reason that college students loved *Cheers* was that we were also struggling to find our place. We were not so much missing our old homes; we were trying to make a new one where we were. The yearning we felt was expressed in the *Cheers* theme song:
>
> "Sometimes you want to go
> Where everybody knows your name."

THE PERILS OF ISOLATION

"The virtuous soul that is alone … is like a lone burning coal. It will grow colder rather than hotter."

John of the Cross

We all need a place to call home, a community where we can really connect. When this is missing from our lives, we suffer from all kinds of maladies harmful to body, mind, and soul.

Body

People who are disconnected from community are at much greater risk of poor health. Isolated persons tend to eat more fast food, be less consistent in sleep patterns, and exercise less than those with close social ties. Yet, even when individuals do everything else right, they are still putting themselves at risk unless they are connected to some kind of community. In his book *Everybody's Normal Till You Get to Know Them,* John Ortberg refers to a study that tracked the habits of seven thousand people for nine years: "Researchers found that the most isolated people were t*hree times more likely to die* than those with strong relational connections. People who had bad health habits (such as smoking, poor eating habits, obesity or alcohol use) but strong social ties lived significantly longer than people who had great health habits but were isolated. In other words, it is better to eat [junk food] with good friends than to eat broccoli alone."[2]

Mind

Individuals who live without the benefit of a supportive community also have higher instances of mental illness. Other people help us keep life in perspective. Without them, we find it much more difficult to get through the hardships of life. Author Anita Diamant writes about a thought-provoking conversation at her local synagogue:

> On Friday night at a typical Oneg Shabbat—a nearly sacramental sharing of decaffeinated coffee, cookies and nontoxic gossip after Friday night services—I was chatting with Andy, a fellow member and pal about whom I remember the basics . . . father of three, a psy-

chiatrist with an impressive C. V. We were talking about the weather, probably, when one of us . . . remarked on a story in the day's newspaper predicting an impending epidemic of depression.

"So, Doctor," I asked, "How do we protect ourselves?" He waved his hand at the scene around us. People chatted in twos and threes, a group stood over the dessert table debating the relative merits of brownies versus lemon squares, a bunch of kids played tag in the sanctuary, awake long past their bedtimes. A burst of laughter rose above the general din. "This," said the doctor, "this is how we protect ourselves."[3]

Soul

Isolated persons tend to struggle more with maladies of the soul. As we have been stating throughout this chapter, when we are disconnected, we feel discontented. We experience a dis-ease that just does not seem to add up. We are in contact with people all through the day, but still we crave relationships. We may find ourselves literally surrounded by crowds of people yet still feel lonely inside. No matter how much money we have or how successful we are, if positive relationships are missing from our lives, there remains a void that cannot be filled.

When Mother Teresa first visited the United States, a well-intentioned reporter asked her if she was enjoying her visit to a country where poverty was not as pervasive as in Calcutta, where she lived and cared for the poor. Mother Teresa responded that while she had not seen the same poverty of body, she had witnessed and despaired over a terrible poverty of soul. She said that in the United States, everywhere she looked, she saw a pervasive loneliness.

"There is hunger for ordinary bread, and there is hunger for love, for kindness, for thoughtfulness; and this is the great poverty that makes people suffer so much."

Mother Teresa

UBUNTU

"Ubuntu refers to the person who is welcoming, who is hospitable, who is warm and generous, who is affirming of others, who ... has a proper self-assurance that comes from knowing they belong in a greater whole, and know that they are diminished when another ... is treated as if they were less than who they are."

Desmond Tutu

How do we break free from the maladies of an isolated existence? The answer does not lie in searching for some mythic place that is already perfectly accepting. Rather, we begin by looking inside. We start by changing the attitudes and habits that inhibit each of us from creating a home for one another in our hearts.

The ancient African notion of *ubuntu* speaks to this increasingly rare ability. *Ubuntu* comes from the Xhosa language of South Africa. It simply means "a way of being together"; but it also speaks of an attitude of mutuality, an openness to other persons that facilitates a healthy interdependence and true community. Someone with *ubuntu* cares about the deepest needs of others. *Ubuntu* does not place emphasis on the lone individual but on the bond that people share in community. It prizes conversation over private reflection, collective wisdom over individual intelligence, and shared lives over solitary existence. *Ubuntu* suggests an alternative way of living in a lonely, disconnected world.

In 1990, an English physicist named Tim Berners-Lee created a software program that allowed physicists on different computers to speak with one another. Berners-Lee insisted that the program operate without royalties. Today his software program is called the World Wide Web, and it is accessible to everyone without cost. We communicate, collaborate, and share through this new way of networking. Before Berners-Lee's creation, individual computers could not "talk" to one another. In creating the World Wide Web, Tim Berners-Lee gave us a brand new way to connect and a whole new reality.

In the same spirit, a free "open source" software appropriately named Ubuntu now exists that allows people to install and use it without cost. Most importantly, it creates a way for people to share their collective experience and expertise to improve the product continually and redistribute it to others. An attitude of *ubuntu* in our lives can provide results similar to the changes in the computer world. When we open our lives to God and other people, a new reality is created for us. We are able to connect in more ways than we ever thought possible. Our lives become "open source"—open to the influence, wisdom, and needs of those around us.

UBUNTU AND CHRISTIAN COMMUNITY

The South African Bishop Desmond Tutu is from the Xhosa people and spent much of his life fighting injustice and apartheid. Drawing from the Xhosa translation of *ubuntu*—that "a person depends on other people to be a person"—Tutu sees a deep affinity between this ancient African idea and Christian *koinonia.* Both traditions extol love and compassion that build community. For Christians, this community is rooted in the biblical account of God's act of Creation in which all persons are created in the image of God. God created human beings because God desired to share a relationship with us. We were created for the primary purpose of communion with God. In Jesus, God revealed such a passion for connecting with us that God came to be with us where we are.

> *"God's Son became human in order that humans would have a home in God."*
>
> *Hildegard of Bingen*

This is who God is. God is the One who desires—above anything else—true community. Our identity, Scripture says, mirrors God's identity. Created in the image of God, we were created for community (Genesis 2). There is something in us— just as there is in our Creator—that yearns for deep, lasting relationships.

This way of thinking about who we are leads to a very different attitude from contemporary assumptions about human identity. We often assume that personal independence should be our ultimate goal, that dependence on other people is a sign of weakness. Recognizing that we all are made in God's image, we begin to see our true identity not as "lone rangers," but as persons called to connect with each other and invited to share a living relationship with our Creator. We are hardwired by God with the longing to belong to our Creator and with each other. These two longings are inescapably entwined. We cannot have communion with God without also living in community together.

> *"It's a mind-blowing concept that the God who created the universe might be looking for company, a real relationship with people."*
>
> *Bono*

LEFT BEHIND

The earliest followers of Jesus Christ, known as the apostles, knew both the longing to belong and the joy of finding God in one another. The Acts of the Apostles tells their story. Acts begins just after Jesus Christ had been raised from the dead. For forty days, the risen Christ was miraculously with his disciples; but then God lifted him up into heaven (Acts 1:1-11). The disciples had no idea what to do. They felt orphaned by the One who had taught them so much. They felt distraught and disconnected from one another.

Then, when they least expected it, the Holy Spirit burst into the world with new power and energy (Acts 2). On the Day of Pentecost, while all the first followers of Jesus Christ were together in

Jerusalem, "suddenly a sound like the blowing of a violent wind came from heaven and filled the whole house where they were sitting. They saw what seemed to be tongues of fire that separated and came to rest on each of them. All of them were filled with the Holy Spirit and began to speak in other tongues as the Spirit enabled them" (Acts 2:2-4).

Empowered by the Holy Spirit, pilgrims who had gathered in Jerusalem from around the world began to hear the good news of Jesus Christ preached in such a way that the message was understood in every language in the world. Peter, assuming a leading role among the followers of Jesus, began to tell the story of Jesus Christ to everyone. People came forward and asked to join the company of the disciples, which included the women who followed Jesus; Jesus' mother, Mary; and Jesus' brothers.

The experience of Pentecost initiated a new way of life for the disciples. They found not only solace and support in one another, but truly a home. Soon thereafter people began to call these early followers of Jesus "Christians," or "Christ-people." But this was not how they saw themselves. They preferred simply to refer to themselves as followers of "the Way" (Acts 9:2). These early Christians saw that together they were embarking on a new adventure. They were entering a new reality, not as individual believers, but as a people who together would follow the same path. No longer orphaned, they found their true home, and their communion with God, in one another. The church of the first century is described as "a people"—those who serve as a flesh-and-blood witness to Jesus Christ. In 1 Peter 2:9-10a we read, "You are a chosen people, a royal priesthood, a holy nation, God's special possession, that you may declare the praises of him who called you out of darkness into his wonderful light. Once you were not a people, but now you are the people of God."

"Pentecost was the . . . originating womb of the Church."
Jason Vickers

GRACIOUS LIVING

"The human soul thrives on . . . the difficult intimacies of belonging."

David Whyte

When Rob, Andy, and Mark were working on this study, they spent a week together in New Orleans. They shared a tour that was given by a native who had lived through Hurricane Katrina. Four months had passed since the hurricane and the resulting flooding had devastated much of the city. The tour guide who showed them around the French Quarter said, "I'm not Catholic, but after the floods I started going to a Catholic church near my home. It was a place to see people, to get news, to be in community." Pausing, she reflected, "You know, I'm still there. I found a place to belong."

What this woman experienced is an example of what Christians call grace. Grace is the pathway that God extends to meet our deep longing for true community. This holy invitation is a response to our deep longing. In *Beginnings: An Introduction to Christian Faith,* we said that our longing for God is matched by God's longing for us. God's longing comes before ours. God goes before us, providing a path back home even before we lose our way. Now we can say even more. God not only longs for us to be in relationship with our Creator; God longs for us to experience true community with our fellow creatures.

Our homesickness is also an opening sign of grace. It suggests that we were made for something more, something better than we typically experience. As we enter the new reality of Christian community, we become people who know God's grace and live in a way that offers grace to others who are also homesick.

"The fellowship of Christians is a gift of grace. . . . Therefore, let anyone who until now has had the privilege of living

a common Christian life with other Christians praise God's grace from the bottom of one's heart."

Dietrich Bonhoeffer

Our salvation in Jesus Christ may be deeply personal, but it is never private. We live out our salvation and grow in grace through our participation in the unique community called church. Becoming a Christian means becoming part of a community of faith and sharing grace with one another. Before Jesus' ascension, the disciples experienced community only through their communion with him. After Pentecost, the disciples experienced communion with Christ through the new community they shared together. Following Jesus Christ is not just about being personally transformed; it is also about being part of a transforming community. Living in community as the body of Christ is about belonging—to God and to other Christians in a fellowship of believers.

THE FIRE OF PENTECOST

The flame is the Christian symbol of Pentecost. Candles on an altar mark the moment when "tongues of fire" descended upon the first followers of Jesus, allowing them to share the gift of God's Spirit regardless of the many different languages they spoke (Acts 2:3). The flame witnesses to God's presence in our midst. This is why most Christians begin their worship services with the lighting of a candle.

Sometimes we overlook the power of this symbol because we forget that fire is essential for our survival. In earlier times, the fireplace was known as the hearth and was the central area for a family or a community. Persons gathered around the hearth to cook the meals they would share or to receive the warmth that was crucial to make it through cold nights. The earliest Christians were no doubt gathered around a fire when they told the stories of Jesus. The hearth was the place where they developed their common memory.

Fire not only gives warmth; it also brings light. Light also is a powerful symbol. Jesus Christ is seen as the light of the world. The Gospel of John describes the incarnation of Jesus with these words: "In him was life, and that life was the light of all people. The light shines in the darkness, and the darkness has not overcome it" (John 1:4-5). When early Christians gathered for prayer, they followed the light. Morning prayer began with the dawning of the sun, and the time for evening prayer was marked by the lighting of lamps. Even today, Christians use a candle and flame to remind ourselves that when we are together, we are also in Christ. We bask in the glow of his light and share in the warmth of his love. Gathered around him, we discover that we truly belong. We belong to each other, and we belong to God. This is where we find our place in the grace of God.

God created the church for a reason: To repair the brokenness of our lives and to equip us to experience life as God intended it to be. We were not created to live alone; we were created to live in community. Only in community will we discover the transformative power of the Holy Spirit. In the world of automobile racing, as developed especially on the NASCAR circuit, successful racers know that two cars working together go faster than either car can go alone. When the car in the lead allows a second car to "draft," the second car hangs just off the bumper. The first car cuts the air for the second car, and the power of the second car pushes forward the first. At our best, we remember that following Jesus is not a solo activity; following Jesus is a team sport. We remember that we are better together than we are on our own.

The church is the instrument through which God brings us back together. It is the community of believers gathered around Jesus Christ. When Jesus referred to himself as "the good shepherd" (John 10:11), perhaps he was not only saying something about himself but also something about how we ought to live. Sheep are not the smartest animals in the world, but even they know it is better not to try to make it on their own. Sheep are rarely attacked in their flock. It is only when they separate from the others and become isolated that they are more vulnerable. The same is true of us, and that is why God called us to be in community. Gathered around the warming fire of God's holy presence, we discover a new identity. We are the flock of the Good Shepherd. This is the answer to our longing to belong.

In the remaining nine sessions, we will describe how both early and contemporary Christians have found a deep sense of belonging through practices that bound them to one another and to God. They have gathered around the fires of nine practices found in Acts 2:41-47. These practices included a ritual washing with water, sharing a meal of bread and wine, praying together, witnessing miraculous signs, sharing possessions, worshiping together, visiting from home to home, resolving conflicts peacefully, and sharing their story with persons outside their community. These are the fires that warm us and shape living in community. Can church still happen today? A friend of Mark and Andy told us this story about a woman named Matice in his church:

> When we asked our usual question, "Why did you come to this church?" Matice responded with passion: "I was fed up with organized religion—up to my chin with churches that exist only for self-preservation. I was invited to attend Christ Church several times over the past two years by my neighbor. When I found out Christ Church had started a program called "Celebrate Recovery" for persons who have hurts, habits, and hang-ups, I thought maybe the church really does care for others. When I started attending, I felt loved and received. I'm here because I think I've found a place to belong."

---

1. Quoted in *Pilgrim in the Ruins: A Life of Walker Percy,* by Jay Tolson (Simon and Schuster, 1992); page 232.

2. From *Everybody's Normal Till You Get to Know Them,* by John Ortberg (Zondervan, 2003); page 33.

3. From *Pitching My Tent: On Marriage, Motherhood, Friendship and Other Leaps of Faith,* by Anita Diamant (Scribner, 2003); page 219.

Two:
How Do We Find Our Place?

Baptism

"Our lives are like islands in the sea, or like trees in the forest, which co-mingle their roots in the darkness underground."
William James

"So those people in Jerusalem who welcomed Simon Peter's message about Jesus Christ were baptized, and on that day of Pentecost about three thousand persons became followers of Jesus Christ. All of these followers of Jesus Christ devoted themselves to the first disciples' teaching and fellowship." (Acts 2:41-42a, authors' paraphrase)

LINE DANCING

One night when Mark was a student at Princeton Seminary, some friends invited him to go dancing. Mark accepted the invitation. Dressed in khakis and oxford shirts, twenty women and men piled into cars and drove forty miles away to a place called the Yellow Rose of New Jersey. When they entered the building, they saw some serious cowboys and cowgirls. The crowd welcomed the awkward strangers from Princeton. Those were the days of country-western line dancing at its best. On the floor, persons were stepping, kicking, sliding, and jumping—all in unison with one another as they listened to "The Electric Slide." At first Mark and his friends stood at the edges of the group. Then a few of Mark's friends jumped in and picked up the rhythm. Although they stepped on a few boot-clad toes, by the end of the evening everyone was line dancing together.

"Do you wanna dance?"
Johnny Rivers

When we are invited to dance and accept the invitation, at first every movement is awkward. Then, slowly but surely, we catch the rhythm. Whether on a ballroom floor, in the sand at the beach, at a nightclub, in a honky-tonk café, or at a rave, when we dance, we are both distinctly individual and yet one with other people. When we catch the rhythm, the dance gradually brings us into a unique social experience. The dance grows until eventually all of us, even the most determined wallflowers, join in this community experience.

BEGINNING TO BELONG

"E Pluribus Unum" (Out of many, one)
Latin motto of The United States of America

Our entry into Christian community has much the same qualities as when we join a dance. Before we learn to move smoothly in community with God and other people, we must accept the invitation to take the first step. For Christians, a crucial first step is baptism.

When we enter into a living community with other followers of Jesus Christ, we have to jump into holy waters if we want to learn, not how to swim, but how to live a Christian life. At that moment we recognize that we are not islands separated from one another; we are more "like trees in the forest, which co-mingle their roots in the darkness underground."[1] Through baptismal water, the Holy Spirit invites us to move in rhythm with the other people around us. Even better, God invites us to join in a sacred dance with the Father Creator, the Son Jesus Christ, and the Holy Spirit.

SPIRITUAL WALLFLOWERS

Many of us, however, perceive ourselves as spiritual wallflowers. We sit out the dance as isolated individuals, feeling that we do not belong. We acts like tourists, sitting up in the balcony as we watch the holy dance unfold before us.

Many of us experience spiritual isolation. One biblical illustration of this appears in the story about the city of Babel (Genesis 11). In this story before time, all the people on the earth spoke the same language. In their unity and especially through their pride, the people of Babel determined that they would build a tower to the heavens; they would work to become like God. Seeing their pride, God took away their ability to speak with one another. When someone asked for a brick or stone, gibberish came forth and no one understood the equest. They failed to complete the tower. Unable to communicate with one another, the people of Babel scattered and formed the multitude of nations we find today. Babel, by definition, means comfusion.

All of us are heirs of that Babel experience. Persons, families, and nations have become displaced and dislocated from one another. Alienated from authentic and intimate relationships with other people and, even worse, separated from God, we feel alone and confused.

Even if we yearn not to be alone, we end up like islands. We live in homes but do not know our next-door neighbors. We work day-in and day-out with coworkers yet know little about their personal lives. We shop in stores where we do not know the names of the clerks. We watch television or surf the Internet alone. We save money for our own retirement because we no longer believe in a social contract in which we all care for our elderly. Even in nuclear families, members take vacations at different times; eat on separate schedules at a variety of places; and socialize with separate groups. Many parents let their young children make their own decisions about when to go to bed, which shows to watch on television, and how to manage their spiritual lives. We assume the authority of each individual to make individual decisions, to "do it my way." We often still live in the age of Babel.

PENTECOST OVER BABEL

The experience of the first disciples and the additional three thousand persons on the Day of Pentecost, however, began to heal the damage of Babel. Through the Holy Spirit, God created a very different kind of community and opened a new way for people to become one with God. The fire of Pentecost became a fire of belonging.

On the Day of Pentecost, through the gift of the Holy Spirit, everyone heard the story of Jesus Christ in his or her own language. Although those people in Jerusalem had come together from every point of the compass and spoke many different languages, everyone could understand the words of the disciples "because each one heard their own language being spoken" (Acts 2:6). Pentecost did not eliminate the diversity of tongues; it provided the followers of Jesus Christ, despite their linguistic, cultural, and even religious distinctions, with the ability to communicate with each other and God in ways never experienced before. Pentecost began to restore the rift of Babel and reunite the children of God, as witnessed by everyone being baptized.

Still today, the community of baptized followers of Jesus Christ serves as an antidote to our social isolation. Think about these contrasting images. Our Western culture emphasizes "I," while the church emphasizes "we." Our contemporary society constructs walls that separate, while the church encourages building bridges that bring persons together. Instead of lone rangers who go it alone and compete with other people, the church uses teams who cooperate. The church invites us not to function as islands, but to be an interconnected forest of trees.

How Do We Find Our Place?

"It's a beautiful day in this neighborhood,
a beautiful day for a neighbor.
Would you be mine?"
Fred M. Rogers

"Yet, how do we join such a community? How can we move from being a wallflower to becoming a dancer? How can we overcome our spiritual isolation to become part of a community bound together by God? Peter's answer, expressed on the day of Pentecost, was to 'repent and be baptized' "

(Acts 2:38a, authors' translation)

THE FIRST STEP: BAPTISM

In the movie *Tender Mercies,*[2] Mac Sledge, a once-famous country-western singer, ends up like the people in many of his songs: divorced, alcoholic, and alone. Mac begins to glimpse a new set of relationships through marriage to a single mother who has a young son. At the end of a long journey of renewal, the new family comes to a rural congregation and a baptismal pool. As a sign of new life beginning, the pastor baptizes the young boy. At the last moment, Mac also steps into the pool. As the family drives home after the service, the boy says, "Well, we've done it, Mac. We're baptized.... Everybody said I was going to feel like a changed person. I guess I do feel a little different, but I don't feel a whole lot different. Do you?" Mac replies, "Not yet." But the restoration has begun.

God acts in our lives even before we are aware of God's presence; but then there comes the time when we do recognize God's presence, hear an invitation to live as God's child, and become a participant in the divine dance. An important first step on the Christian journey involves baptism. Like Alice's rabbit hole, baptism stands as the doorway into a new relationship with other people; a new relationship with God; and even a new reality. As in C. S. Lewis' *The Lion, the Witch, and the Wardrobe,* before the four children got to the magical land of Narnia, they first had to pass through an ordinary-looking clothing wardrobe.

Imagine that your Christian journey is like visiting the home of a friend. As you approach your destination, you see the house from a distance. You park your car, walk up the steps, approach the front door, and knock. Only when your friend opens the door and you cross the threshold have you truly entered the home. In our spiritual journey, baptism operates as that front door into the community of Christians.

Andy was baptized when he was five months old. On Palm Sunday morning in 1953, his parents brought him to the congregation where they had met and then married, a place where they felt they truly belonged. The congregation that morning included three of Andy's grandparents, five uncles and aunts, and a handful of cousins. After the sermon, the Reverend Charlie Bowles invited Andy's family, plus four other infants and their families, to the front of the congregation. One by one, Bowles sprinkled water on the head of each child and said, "I baptize you in the name of the Father, the Son, and the Holy Spirit." After the service was over, Andy's family carried him to his grandmother's house for a feast together. The rest of Andy's life has been living out what happened to him that morning.

"Baptism points back to the work of God, and forward to the life of faith."

J. Alec Motyer

A SACRAMENT OF BELONGING

"You can trust us to stick with you through thick and thin—to the bitter end. . . . But you cannot trust us to let you face trouble alone, and go off without a word. We are your friends, Frodo."

Merry the Hobbit

Baptism is the first step in the divine dance. Through baptism, we recognize that we are God's children every moment of our lives. The washing with water affirms God's love that has always been present and available to each one of us and for every person everywhere. From that moment on, we can never forget that we are in community with other followers of Jesus Christ and with God. In this sacrament of belonging, the church says to us, "You belong."

A long time ago, warriors from another nation pursued a band of Lakota braves. The Lakotas found themselves standing on the banks of a raging river. Hemmed in by the torrent of water on one side and surrounded by their enemy on the other, the Lakota feared that they would die. How could they be saved? The smaller men climbed onto the shoulders of the larger men, and everyone locked arms with one another. The whole company waded in unison into the rapids. The weight and stability of the Lakotas together enabled them to cross the treacherous waters. Linking arms together and stepping into the water saved them all.

> *"Faith is not me and God alone. Baptism puts me in a community of believers. Though they can be irritating, exasperating and occasionally cruel, they continually teach me that to love others means loving—and forgiving—those who can be unlovable. . . . Without such outward expressions, I can easily become obsessed with self. . . . I stay connected to church because it connects me with the One who loves me, and compels me to do the same for others."*
>
> *Tom Schaefer*

THE WATER BATH

> *"Christianity is about water. . . . It's about full immersion, about falling into something elemental and wet. Most of what we do in worldly life is geared toward our staying dry, looking good, not going under. But in baptism, in lakes and rain and tanks and*

fonts, you agree to do something that's a little sloppy because at that same time it's also holy, and absurd. It's about surrender, giving in to all those things we can't control; it's a willingness to let go of balance and decorum and get drenched."

Anne Lamott

We drink water, bathe in water, and play in water. In Genesis and in science, we read that life began in a caldron of water. Each of us was formed in the waters of our mothers' wombs. Our human bodies are 98% water. When we look for signs of life on other planets, we first look for water. As water stands at the center of life itself, through water we also enter the community of God's people. Water signifies our new birth as followers of Jesus Christ and our new life together in community.

Deep within us, we yearn to reclaim the power of water to restore us to life. As Marilynne Robinson wrote in her novel *Gilead*:

> A few years ago . . . I was walking up to the church. There was a young couple strolling along half a block ahead of me. The sun had come up brilliantly after a heavy rain, and the trees were glistening and very wet. On some impulse, plain exuberance, I suppose, the fellow jumped up and caught hold of a branch, and a storm of luminous water came pouring down on the two of them, and they laughed and took off running, the girl sweeping water off her hair and her dress as if she were a little bit disgusted, but she wasn't. It was a beautiful thing to see, like something from a myth. I don't know why I thought of that now, except perhaps because it is easy to believe in such moments that water was made primarily for blessing, and only secondarily for growing vegetables or doing the wash.[3]

At the time of Pentecost, baptism was not a new ritual. Faithful Jews practiced baptism as a ritual of purification and a sign of holiness. Out in the desert beside the Jordan River, John the Baptist practiced baptism for the repentance of sins (Mark 1). John baptized Jesus, and then Jesus asked his followers to do the same. Baptism grew in meaning and became the sign of God's new relationship with the followers of Jesus Christ. When the people on the Day of Pentecost asked Peter what the next step of their journey together ought to include, Peter invited them, "Be baptized" (Acts 2:38).

As persons step forward to respond to God's invitation to be in community, water provides the entrance into the community of the faithful in many ways. A young couple brings their child forward for baptism. A youth professes Jesus Christ as Savior and is confirmed. A congregation reaffirms the baptismal covenant through vows and blessings with water. An older man enters a sanctuary, touches some holy water in a small bowl, and lifts the water to his forehead in the sign of a cross. All these actions demonstrate that we today continue a sacred dance of belonging begun by the first Jerusalem congregation.

BAPTISMAL IMAGES

God has always used water as a sign of love and of bringing people into *ubuntu*. God created the waters of the heavens and earth (Genesis 1), saved the Hebrews in their flight from Egypt through the Red Sea, provided water in their wilderness journey, led them through the Jordan River, (Exodus), and saved Jonah by means of a giant fish (Jonah). The first Christians shared stories about these divine uses of water and through their own actions gave water an even deeper meaning.

Baptism's many layers of meaning are simple and complex, as well as tactile and mysterious. Just as water can exist as a liquid, gas, or solid, baptism also has many realities, no one of which ever fully explains the ritual.

For example, the apostle Paul claimed that at one level baptism involves union with Jesus Christ and his death and resurrection: "Don't you know that all of us who were baptized into Christ Jesus were baptized into his death? We were therefore buried with him through baptism into death in order that, just as Christ was raised from the dead through the glory of the Father, we too may live a new life" (Romans

6:3-4). No longer are we individuals, our old selves, or islands; instead we have become intimately connected with God, made new, and brought into the forest. Baptism means so much more, however.

At another level, baptism, like a bath or shower, has cleansing power. As John baptized people in the Jordan River for the forgiveness of their sins, baptism washes away the failures of our lives (Acts 2:38; 1 Corinthians 6:11b). Baptism cleanses us of our self-centeredness, present from the moment of our birth, and refocuses our attention on our relationship with God. Based on this cleansing image, some Christians remember their baptism every time they take a shower or bath.

At yet another level, baptism has a more institutional meaning. Through baptism we are adopted into the people of God; thus it serves as a rite of initiation (1 Corinthians 12:13; Galatians 3:27-28). In the Old Testament, God instructed Abraham to circumcise male infants as a sign of God's promise to make them the chosen people (Genesis 17:1-14). Through baptism, we believe we become heirs of God's promise to Abraham and members of the church universal. This level reminds us that Christians are not born but made. Our birth into a Christian family does not assure us that we necessarily become followers of Jesus Christ. Each of us individually must hear and respond to God's invitation through water. At baptism, the church adopts each one of us into the family of God and assumes new obligations toward us. Likewise, as we assume our rightful place in the church family, we also recognize our obligations to that family. Because of these understandings, most baptisms take place in the midst of an entire congregation.

> *"Being baptized, we are enlightened; being enlightened, we are adopted as child; being adopted, we are made perfect; being made complete, we are made immortal.... This work has many names: gift of grace, enlightenment, perfection, washing."*
>
> *Clement of Alexandria*

At still another level, baptism involves our eternal lives, offering each of us the promise of new life (2 Corinthians 5:17; Titus 3:5). For example, Jesus said to the Samaritan woman, "Everyone who drinks this water will be thirsty again, but those who drink the water I give them will never thirst. Indeed, the water I give them will become in them a spring of water welling up to eternal life" (John 4:13-14). When we are baptized, we have become so intimately connected to God that not even death can end that relationship. Thus, the last chapter of the final book of the Bible, the Revelation of John, opens with this baptismal image: "the river of the water of life, as clear as crystal, flowing from the throne of God and of the Lamb down the middle of the great street of the city. On each side of the river stood the tree of life" (Revelation 22:1-2).

BAPTISMAL ISSUES

"The church must recover the generative power of baptism. Baptism ... means entry into a stream of promise that is free but not cheap.... Latent in this thick moment of holy vows ... we watch the splash of the holy water and hear the uncompromising name of the irascible Maker of promises."

Walter Brueggemann

Many traditions practice baptism differently, from the gentle sprinkling of a newborn child to washing in flowing rivers to the full immersion of adults. Throughout the ages, however, Christians have understood that the effectiveness of baptism does not depend upon how much water is used, where the water is placed, the age or faith of the person, the character of the pastor, which words are used, or the practices of a local congregation. God alone, through the Holy Spirit, makes the baptism effective.

While we may forget, neglect, or even defy our baptism, God never does. While we may not remember the details of the day of our baptism, or believe that we have rejected God's presence in our lives, or have a new experience of God, God's power makes baptism eternally effective for us. Because of God's faithfulness, when we wish to celebrate our response to God's love, we do not rebaptize one another but instead reaffirm our commitment to God through a blessing with water.

Baptism stands as a powerful witness to God's invitation for us to participate in a new reality, to join the holy dance, and to belong to a new community. In baptism we remember the life, death, and resurrection of Jesus Christ. As the waters wash away our sins, the church welcomes us into community and identifies us as followers of Jesus. All Christians in every age, in every place, and in every time—Baptists to Russian Orthodox to Pentecostals to Lutherans to Presbyterians to United Methodists—are part of the living body of Christ through baptism. Every member of every congregation is a part of the worldwide church. Pentecost overwhelms Babel.

Andy remembers a young girl, baptized several years before, who was at the baptism of her little brother:

> I spoke with the girl before the service and told her that I was about to wash her brother like I had once baptized her. During the baptism, this child stood beside the baptismal font, fascinated by the water, and watching carefully as I poured water on her brother's head and then marked his forehead with the sign of the cross. After the service, the sister came over to me, pulled up her long bangs of hair, and asked, "Is my cross still there?" My answer had to be, "Yes, the cross is still there." Baptism had marked her with an invisible but indelible sign that would change her life.

Yet, baptism means even more than all this. Baptism not only changes us and our relationship with other people in the community of the church; it also changes our relationship with God.

BAPTISM AND THE THREE-IN-ONE GOD

"When we are baptized into the community in the name of the Trinity, our lives become relational in a more thoroughgoing and deeper way than ever, not only with God but the membership of the baptized."

Eugene Peterson

Our most sacred dance does not just intermingle our roots with other people in the church; it also molds our relationship with God. Baptism unites us with God and invites us to participate in a larger world that reflects the mystery of the Father, the Son, and the Holy Spirit. Baptism immerses us in the three-in-one God.

In Richard Lischer's memoir, *Open Secrets,* he described his first congregation, Cana Lutheran Church, in rural Illinois: "In Cana we baptized our babies, celebrated marriages, wept over the dead, and received Holy Communion—all by the light of our best window." [4] The best window in Cana Lutheran Church was a stained glass window installed high above the Communion Table. The center of the window displayed one word *Deus* (God). The word was enclosed in a triangle containing three words: *Pater, Filius,* and *Spiritus Sanctus* (Father, Son, and Holy Spirit). Whenever that congregation celebrated a high-holy moment in their life together, they did so under the warm glow and multicolored light of that window and in the reality of the God to whom the window pointed.[5]

At the very end of his ministry, Jesus told his disciples that one of their major tasks was to baptize persons "in the name of the Father and of the Son and of the Holy Spirit" (Matthew 28:19). Following his instruction, from the Day of Pentecost on, new Christians have been baptized with those words.

The implications of using these names of God at our baptism are enormous. Through baptism we become participants in the company of the God who creates all that exists, the God who enters history and establishes salvation, and the God who forms a community to worship and to serve the world. When we hear the three names of God at our baptism, we are welcomed as full participants in every aspect of God.

THE TRINITY

The Trinity, a summary description of God as revealed in the Bible, while not found in the Bible itself, stands at the center of Christian thought. Tertullian, a lay teacher of the second century, was the first person we know of to use the word *Trinity* to describe the biblical richness and diversity of who God is and how God relates to us. By using this word, Tertullian sought to make the point that from all eternity God is one, but also God is not alone.

Some people think that the Trinity is an unnecessary complexity. In its most basic form, the Trinity sounds anti-rational, like bad arithmetic. How can God be one yet somehow also three? This mysterious math sounds similar to what we declare at a Christian marriage: In marriage two persons become one. How can we add up all these figures to give us a correct answer?

The truth is that we experience God in so many different ways that only using one term cannot capture God's fullness. We know God the Father as Creator of all things. When we look at the beauty of the world with awe and wonder, we instinctively whisper our praise to the gracious One who started it all. We know God the Son as the Word at the beginning of Creation, the child born in Bethlehem, the teacher, the miracle worker, and the One who triumphed over death. We know God the Holy Spirit as the One who moved upon the waters at Creation and blessed the disciples on the Day of Pentecost. Throughout the Bible and all around us, we discover glimpses of God the Father, God the Son, and God the Holy Spirit.

A fourth-century preacher, Athanasius, said that the true essence of God is found in the very relationship of Father, Son, and Spirit. Athanasius believed that to be a person is to be in relationship with another person. Because God is personal, God must necessarily be relational. Athanasius refused to reduce God to a math problem or to define God only within our human logic. The Trinity reminds us that God, though transcendent, is also inherently relational and emphatically personal.

The Trinity affirms that at the center of the universe and from the beginning of time, God existed as a loving, perfect community. Yet, God yearned for even more, desiring to expand the community and invite others into the sacred dance. So we were created in the image and likeness of God. Part of our likeness to God includes our need to be in community with other people, to belong to God and all of creation. If we try to live solitary, independent lives, we will never be fully human. Being alone goes against the way God created us to live. God created us to belong in relationship. Baptism signifies this intimate connection with God. The one-yet-three God is a God of infinite surprises who yearns to be in loving relationship with all of us. God ultimately wants to belong to us and wants for us to belong to God.

> *"The Trinity is not a mystery that keeps us in the dark, but a mystery in which we are taken by the hand and gradually led into the light, a light to which our souls are not yet accustomed, but light nevertheless, in which we recognize ourselves as persons in the company of a personal God . . . and develop . . . a not-knowing in the presence of the God who knows us."*
>
> *Eugene Peterson*

BOUND TOGETHER

Baptism invites each of us into an intimate relationship with other followers of Jesus Christ and with our three-in-one God. Through water and the Spirit, we are connected to one another, experience a whole new set of relationships, and receive the gift of life. When we respond to the invitation to participate, we join in a holy dance.

Andy caught a glimpse of the breath and scope of our baptismal relationships in one of his congregations:

> One Sunday morning, in our predominately Anglo congregation in North Carolina, a new family appeared at morning worship. We knew that they were new because their skin was black, they cut their hair differently, and they wore African clothing. After worship, the father, mother, and son remained to visit. They were new residents in our community and had walked two miles to our facilities. As the father, William, said, "We were baptized as Christians in Ghana. We have been taught that when we need assistance, we should first go to our family in Jesus Christ." William had just lost his job, and their family was in crisis. Their biological family lived thousands of miles away, so they appealed to other baptized Christians for help.
>
> Our congregation helped William find a job and purchased a car and furniture for the family. Over the next few years, this African family became a vital part of our congregation. Nora, the wife and mother, helped teach vacation Bible school. Kojo, the son, entered our preschool. When William and Nora gave birth to their next child, Esther, my family welcomed the family into our home during Esther's first weeks of life. When the time came to baptize Esther, excitement built; and her baptismal day became a major celebration for the whole congregation. As we poured water onto the head of Esther in the name of the Father, the Son, and the Holy Spirit, she gurgled and smiled underneath her wet hair. Across the ocean and spanning two continents, baptism had brought us together as the family of Jesus Christ. We all belonged to one another and to the three-in-one God. The divine dance had begun.

---

1. William James quoted in *Sunbeams: A Book of Quotations,* edited by Sy Safransky (North Atlantic Books, 1990): page 5.
2. From *Tender Mercies,* screenplay by Horton Foote (1984).
3. From *Gilead,* by Marilynne Robinson (Farrar, Straus & Girous, 2004); pages 27–28.
4. From *Open Secrets: A Spiritual Journey Through a Country Church,* by Richard Lischer (Doubleday, 2001); page 81.
5. From *Open Secrets: A Spiritual Journey Through a Country Church,* by Richard Lischer; page 81.

Three:
What Are We Hungry For?

Holy Communion

"Ain't nobody like to be alone
Everybody's got a hungry heart."
Bruce Springsteen

"They devoted themselves to . . . the holy meal of bread and cup."

(Acts 2:42, authors' paraphrase)

"So whether you eat or drink or whatever you do, do it all for the glory of God."

(1 Corinthians 10:31)

EATING TOGETHER

What makes human beings different from other animals? Many theories have been advanced. Some scholars believe that our use of tools, language, and fire differentiates us from other living creatures. Richard Wrangham, a Harvard professor of anthropology in a field called paleo-gastronomy, declares that the answer is cooking an evening meal! Cooking, common in all human cultures, binds persons into the human family. In every age and in every society, a hot meal in the evening "is universal and central to human life."[1] Sharing food together makes us human and also unites us with the Father, the

Son, and the Holy Spirit who created us all. The fire of Pentecost brings us together around the fire of a holy meal.

When the early Christians gathered after Pentecost, one of their first actions was to share in a meal of bread and wine. As they ate and drank together, they came into community with each other and with the risen Jesus Christ. In sharing a common meal, the first Christians declared that they and all Christians everywhere and at all times are one body. Throughout history and still today, when Christians gather together, we find a place of belonging by eating the bread of life and drinking from the cup of salvation.

EATING ALONE

Many people today do not know how to eat together. We often eat our meals alone, from burgers and fries to nachos and tacos to beef and broccoli to kimchi and pork to pizza. In sushi bars, people sit side by side but often dine alone. Visit any restaurant and notice how many people sit by themselves. Even communal meals demonstrate our separateness. Watch when families go out to eat at the same restaurant together: Everyone orders a different food. Mom has a vegetable plate, Dad eats a steak, one child has a cheese pizza, and the other child orders a pile of chicken fingers. Even when we eat together, we eat separately.

The National Center on Addiction and Substance Abuse has conducted studies showing that whether we eat together indicates the quality of our lives. When teenagers have dinner with their families at least five times a week, as compared with youth who do not, they are significantly less likely to exhibit destructive behaviors such as drug use or cigarette smoking or to have low grades in school. Yet, most teens eat less than this number of meals with their family.

"You satisfy the hungry heart, with gift of finest wheat.
Come, give to us, O saving Lord, the bread of life to eat."
Omer Westerdorf

Compare the above findings with experiences in another era of history. Andy remembers:

> As I was growing up, my parents, three brothers, and I ate almost all our meals at home around our kitchen table. We each had our own place at the table. My mother always offered us two food options: the food she prepared or nothing. These meals brought us closer as a family and closer to friends who occasionally joined us at our table.
>
> On special occasions, we would pack up our car with a variety of foods and drive an hour away to celebrate family meals at the home of my maternal great-grandmother in rural North Carolina. The old Lambeth Home, built in 1852, survived the Civil War and still remains within our family. Minnie, my great-grandmother, hosted the meal and set the tables with the finest china and silver, plus every other glass, plate, and utensil in the house. Four generations of family gathered from the kitchen to the living room around tables full of meats, vegetables, breads, biscuits, and desserts. A blessing would be prayed. Children were served first, but due to limited chairs we sat on the steps or in the yard outside. Adults then filled their plates and sat at the "adult tables." As we shared this meal together, we visited with each other and bonded in ways that sustained us until the next feast.

EARLY EATING DISORDERS

Division around the table, though prevalent today, is not new. Some of the Christians in the very first decades of the church forgot the primary meaning of the meal: community. Paul, who created many of the first churches throughout the Roman Empire, discovered that the holy meal could be divisive. In the Greek city of Corinth, where one of the first congregations outside the Holy Land was established, the members of the new Christian congregation struggled with how to eat together. While all the people heard the same Scripture read and preached, when it came time for the meal, the rich people who brought the most food ate in one area and the poor people who brought little or nothing ate in another area. The rich people ate the finest wheat bread and drank luxury wines, sometimes becoming drunk; the poor people had crumbs and water.

In Paul's first letter to the Corinthian Christians, he challenged the new followers of Jesus to remember that the meal was to bring them together. Paul wrote, "Is not the cup of thanksgiving for which we give thanks a participation in the blood of Christ? And is not the bread that we break a participation in the body of Christ? Because there is one loaf, we, who are many, are one body, for we all partake of the one loaf. . . . So whether you eat or drink or whatever you do, do it all for the glory of God" (1 Corinthians 10:16-17, 31).

A COMMON MEAL

Why was Paul so upset with the practices of the Corinthians? He was so upset because their actions violated the essential truth of the holy meal, our unity with one another. Gathered around a table and sharing food with one another, the Christian community serves as an antidote to our individualistic culture that encourages eating alone. Congregational covered-dish and potluck dinners remind us of those first feasts after the Day of Pentecost. Love feasts, Sunday school picnics, Wednesday night dinners, and pancake breakfasts help us belong to one another. When we share a loaf of bread and a cup of wine, Jesus Christ truly becomes present in our midst.

The concept of a common meal stood in sharp contrast to the culture out of which Christianity arose. Roman authorities did not practice eating with the people whose lands they occupied. Many Jews at that time believed that no Jew could eat at a meal with a Greek without incurring ceremonial defilement. At mealtime each group retreated to its own exclusive enclave. We find echoes of this practice in Shakespeare's play *The Merchant of Venice*. In one scene, the moneylender Shylock says, "I will buy with you, sell with you, talk with you, walk with you, and so following; but I will not eat with you, drink with you, nor pray with you."[2] Many cultures then and now insist that each family, each group, and each sect should eat alone.

In contrast, followers of Jesus Christ sought to end social divisions and welcome everyone to the table. Especially when the new Christian community shared in bread and cup, they welcomed people from every corner of the compass to join them in their feast. Eating and drinking together, they became one people and believed that Jesus Christ served as host.

ORIGINS OF THE MEAL

What meals formed the background of the Christian feast? When the ancient Hebrews were held as slaves in Egypt, Moses led the people out through the sea to the Promised Land (Exodus). The people left quickly, leaving behind most of their belongings; but the one thing they took with them was bread that was unleavened (had not yet risen). When their own bread ran out in the desert, God provided them a different kind of bread, which the people called "manna," with the taste of coriander seed. Later, when the people of Israel came into the Promised Land, they remembered their exodus and survival in the celebration of Passover. An important part of that celebration is the meal called a Seder, complete with unleavened matzo bread.

As Jesus journeyed through the Holy Land, much of his ministry involved meals. He ate with his friends (Matthew 9:9-11), told about a family reunion feast that a loving father provided for his wayward son (Luke 15:11-24), fed 5,000 people on a lonely hillside (John 6:1-14), shared a meal with the tax collector Zacchaeus (Luke 19:1-10), and ate in the home of Mary and Martha (Luke 10:38-42). Then, on the night before his death, Jesus ate a Passover meal (Matthew 26:26-29)—a feast of lamb, grapes, and rich wines with his friends.

Three days later, on the day of his resurrection, Jesus again broke bread with two followers at Emmaus (Luke 24:13-35). Not even death could destroy the emerging Christian community, which had been formed through meals together.

> *"The source of all such coming together is surely Jesus himself. Community is ever his gift. It was this way from the start. He formed the table fellowship.... When he came upon them after the Resurrection, he joined two on the road, encouraged a frightened crew huddled behind locked doors, fed a hungry band of them at dawn on the shores of Galilee. He initially had drawn persons together, and he continued to shape them as a body. When the Holy Spirit burned forth Pentecost, it settled not on one but on a whole assembly.... In Christ Jesus we are formed into one people stretching through the ages of time. And in this sense, the community he creates is not only a gift. It is holy. That is, its source is not in us. It emanates from him. Community sweeps forth and claims us from the realms of grace."*
>
> *Stephen Doughty*

When the new community formed on the Day of Pentecost, it was natural that the new Christians gathered for a communal feast. Early Christians primarily distinguished themselves from their Jewish cousins by worshiping on the first day of the week (Sunday) to remember the resurrection of Jesus from the dead) and by celebrating this special meal. When we celebrate the holy meal, we recall the Exodus, the Passover meal, the communal meals of Jesus' ministry, the Last Supper in the upper room, and the meals that Jesus shared with his friends after his resurrection. This meal reminds us that the word *companion* comes from a French word meaning "one with whom one shares bread."

A HOLY MYSTERY

What was so holy about the simple action of breaking a loaf of bread and drinking from one cup? Why do Christians in every community still gather for this ritual? Most simply, in this holy meal we vividly and actively remember Jesus Christ. As he said, "Do this in remembrance of me" (Luke 22:19). We eat and drink together because Jesus told us to. But what does our memory invoke? What does this meal mean?

One way to understand the meal is to describe its basic elements. Bread and wine are served from the table, which may be called an altar, Communion Table, altar-table, or the Lord's Table. The table reminds us of both a family meal where all face one another (Luke 22:14) and the altar of sacrifice of Jesus Christ (1 Corinthians 5:7b).

The bread may be leavened (bread with yeast) or unleavened (like the bread of the Exodus), ideally large enough for everyone to share the same loaf. Jesus called himself "the bread of life" (John 6:25-59).

At the meal we also share the fruit of the vine: wine. In the Old Testament, the blood of a sacrificial animal ratified an agreement between God and worshipers (Exodus 12:12-28). In the New Testament, Jesus said that his blood shed on the cross would shape a new relationship between people and God (Mark 14:23-24).

Another way to understand the meal is by looking at the basic actions within the service itself: take, bless, break, and give. These actions repeat the actions of Jesus, provide structure for the worship service, and outline a model of how Christians live together for the world. As Jesus Christ took the bread and cup, so the pastor or worship leader prepares the meal on the table; and we remember that God takes us as we are. As Christ blessed the bread and wine, so the pastor offers these elements to God in praise; and God blesses each one of us. As Jesus broke the bread, so does the leader; and God breaks us from our self-centeredness and isolation. As Jesus Christ gave the bread and wine to his friends, so the loaf and cup are shared in a congregation; and we are asked to share ourselves with all creation.

> *"When the eucharist is served, a reshaping of human society begins.... Communion is a microcosm of the service as a whole. The elements of bread and wine are taken, blessed, broken and shared just as Jesus was taken, blessed, broken and shared. In a similar way the congregation as a whole is taken out of its ordinary pursuits; blessed with the grace and truth of forgiveness and scripture; broken in the disciplines of intercession, peace-making and food-sharing; and shared with the world in love and service. As the bread and the wine are offered, transformed and received, the congregation, and through it the whole creation, is offered, transformed and received.... The breaking of the bread may be the most poignant act of worship."*
>
> *Samuel Wells*

ONE MEAL, MANY NAMES

Other meanings of this holy meal can be found in its many names. *The Lord's Supper* reminds us that Jesus Christ invites us to the table and hosts the meal. While a pastor or leader of the congregation presides at the table, we believe that Jesus Christ himself serves as the host. *Holy Communion* focuses on the community found between the people and God and between the people and each other. In the meal we re-establish our links with the community of all Christians and with God; as Paul wrote, "Because there is one loaf, we, who are many, are one body, for we all partake of the one loaf" (1 Corinthians 10:17). *Eucharist* comes from the Greek word for "thanksgiving," reminding us to give thanks to God for the feast for the love of God that formed the faith of that early community (see Acts 2:46-47a). *Sacrifice* invokes another theme of the meal, as we re-present on the table or altar Jesus

Christ as he offers himself for the forgiveness of our sins (Hebrews 9:26). As Paul wrote, "For Christ, our Passover lamb, has been sacrificed" (1 Corinthians 5:7b). Finally, but not exhaustively, the *Heavenly Banquet* possesses a foretaste of the feast that we will all celebrate with God in heaven (Matthew 26:29; Mark 14:25). One day all of us will gather at a great feast in the New Jerusalem.

Such names and explanations, however, have their limits. Ultimately, our worship and especially Holy Communion and baptism can never be "explained." Every time we come to the table of our Savior, we discover something new about God, ourselves, and our relationship with God and other people.

Because of the rich meaning of this meal, Holy Communion, along with baptism, is known as a "sacrament." The Latin word *sacramentum* means "promise" or "vow," showing that in these actions Jesus Christ promises to be with us. The original word for sacrament in the Bible was *mysterion* or "mystery," indicating that in these acts God discloses a relationship with us that exceeds rational explanation. Both baptism and Holy Communion express to us beyond words and actions the love of the Father, Son, and Holy Spirit; through them God "shows and tells" us that we are God's children. The sacraments make visible God's love and relationship with us.

"Come, sinners, to the gospel feast,
let every soul be Jesus' guest.
You need not one be left behind,
for God hath bid all humankind."
Charles Wesley

EATING DISORDERS TODAY

Unfortunately, the many different traditions for Holy Communion tend to divide us from one another. Just as there are many understandings of and practices of baptism, so, too, many people debate and may divide over questions about Holy Communion. For example, Who presides at the table? Which words are used? What kind of bread is offered? Is the cup filled with wine or with grape juice? Who is welcome to receive? Most significantly, Where is Jesus in the sharing of the bread and cup? Partly because of disagreements about the precise answers to all these questions, Christians have divided into various denominations and sects. One of the greatest scandals of the church universal is that the meal, which was meant to bring us together and remind us that we belong to one another, has instead divided us.

> *"The symbolism and power of the Eucharist change how we think about food, the breaking of bread, and who is welcome at the table. Once we have broken bread at the Lord's table, we cannot help but take bread out to those who have no bread at all."*
>
> *James Howell*

We also remain divided in terms of whom we choose to welcome to the table and whom we turn away. Do our table actions, either intentionally or unintentionally, restrict access to the bread and wine? For example, we must remember and accommodate those who because of age, illness, imprisonment, or transportation cannot be present when we serve the meal. Hospitals, nursing homes, private homes of shut-ins, hospices, prisons, and custodial institutions are filled with people who yearn to share at a common table with Christians. How do we involve them in our family meal? Even further, what about the people who believe themselves to be unworthy to eat at our table: the poor, the victims of prejudice, and other persons who are neglected or oppressed? Jesus Christ invited these kinds of people to eat with him. To be faithful to the holy mystery, we must do the same.

COMING TOGETHER AROUND THE TABLE

In the movie *Places in the Heart,* an odd assortment of Texans slowly become a community during the Great Depression in the 1930s. The movie introduces us to, among others, a sheriff who is accidentally shot dead, the African American youth who shot the sheriff and is lynched, the sheriff's widow, her two young children, an African American handyman who helps the widow keep her farm, a couple in a damaged marriage, a greedy banker and mill owner, and a blind boarder. The movie weaves all of their lives together. Then, in the powerful closing scene, Holy Communion is shared in a tiny, whitewashed, clapboard church. As a tray of tiny Communion cups is passed down each aisle, we see everyone—including people who have died—receiving the bread and wine. All of them are together, giving this movie moment the feel of the heavenly banquet.

> "Then Levi held a great banquet for Jesus at his house, and a large crowd of tax collectors and others were eating with them. But the Pharisees and the teachers of the law who belonged to their sect complained to his disciples, 'Why do you eat and drink with tax collectors and sinners?' Jesus answered them, 'It is not the healthy who need a doctor, but the sick. I have not come to call the righteous, but sinners to repentance.' "
>
> (Luke 5:29-32)

Because all of us hunger for communion with God and other people, we should always strive vigorously to open the holy meal to everyone. However, our hunger is so great that sometimes we guard the meal too jealously. In the first congregation Andy served as pastor, three-year-old Christy was a beautiful, blue-eyed blonde. She was full of life. As she walked through the halls, everyone turned to greet her and she would stop to hug them. On Andy's first Sunday in the congregation:

I invited everyone to come to the table and receive the holy meal. Christy, holding her parents' hands, came forward. I assumed (incorrectly, I would later discover) that all the children received the bread and cup. I handed Christy a large piece of bread and said to her, "This is the body of Jesus for you, Christy." I then offered her a one-swallow-size cup filled with grape juice. I said, "Christy, this is the blood of Jesus for you." Christy reverently ate and drank.

At the end of the service, I greeted Christy's parents at the back of the sanctuary. They explained to me that this was the first time Christy had ever received Holy Communion. As we speculated about what she had experienced, we heard a squeal from the front of the sanctuary. Christy had run to the table and was stuffing her face with bread, saying out loud, "The body of Jesus for Christy." She also was drinking down as many small cups of grape juice as she could, repeating my words, "The blood of Jesus for Christy." Christy had experienced Jesus Christ in the Holy Meal, and she could not get enough. The adults were appalled, but Christy understood the love of God.

Saints and sinners, young babies and older adults, members of a congregation and first-time guests, those confident of their relationship with Jesus and those who are uncertain—all find room at the table of Jesus Christ. Whether we are rich or poor, male or female, or of any color under the rainbow, Jesus welcomes each of us into community with one another.

"The Lord's Supper is fellowship with Christ, and so fellowship with other Christians; their common union with Christ naturally leads to a union of those who share the Lord's Supper, a communion of Christians among themselves."

Hans Küng

UNITY IN DIVERSITY

"Bread eaten by oneself is physical, but bread shared with another is spiritual."

Mahatma Gandhi

We are heirs of the Pentecost community. For two thousand years, Christians have gathered at a table to create community anew. All of us long to belong to a community of people who share at a table together. God knows that we cannot live our lives in quiet separation from one another. We are not islands. We are not solitary individuals. Across the years, among different cultures, for different people with a variety of memories, with different hurts and many dreams, we learn to recognize our essential connection with God and with one another through this holy meal. We all are invited to the table to be one with each other and one with Christ Jesus, at a place where we all belong.

Years ago, Andy went with several youth from his congregation to lead worship at a retirement home. When they arrived, there were about thirty residents in the activity room. About half of the women and men could walk in by themselves, but other residents arrived in wheelchairs. A number of residents had Alzheimer's disease. Most of the residents could not hear well, and a number of them had difficulty speaking. Some of them had dressed up for worship. Andy remembers:

> We walked around the room, shook hands, and greeted everyone. We sang several old hymns that everyone knew by heart, including "Amazing Grace." We had struggled during the week about how to lead the service and then decided to celebrate Holy Communion. Everyone could participate; and the actions of taking, blessing, breaking, and giving would speak louder than any words. I took a loaf of bread and a large cup, blessed the bread and wine, and broke the bread. While the youth served the bread and cup, our youth told the residents in turn that God loved them. One woman began to cry. She said aloud, "It has been years since I received Holy Communion." Although her short-term memory was gone, she remembered the power of the holy meal with Jesus. Even though we did not know her, we discovered that we were in community together.

1. From "Cooking Makes Us Far Less Beastly," in *The Charlotte Observer,* April 20, 2005; page E-1.

2. From *The Merchant of Venice,* i, 3, 36-38, by William Shakespeare.

* For several views of Holy Communion, see *This Holy Mystery: A United Methodist Understanding of Holy Communion* (The General Board of Discipleship, 2003, 2004); *The Book of Common Prayer* (Episcopal, 1979); *The Lutheran Book of Worship* (Augsburg Fortress, 1978); *Moravian Book of Worship* (1995); *The Book of Common Worship* (Presbyterian Church, U.S.A., Westminster/John Knox Press, 1993); and *The Book of Worship: United Church of Christ* (1986).

Four: What Happens When We Pray Together?

Prayer

"Prayer is the language of Christian community. In prayer the nature of community becomes visible because in prayer we direct ourselves to the One who forms the community.... Together we pray to God, who calls us and makes us into a new people. Praying is not one of the many things a community does. Rather, it is its very being."

Henri Nouwen

"They devoted themselves to ... prayer."
(Acts 2:42)

"I thank my God every time I remember you. In all my prayers for all of you, I always pray with joy because of your partnership in the gospel from the first day until now, being confident of this, that he who began a good work in you will carry it on to completion until the day of Christ Jesus. It is right for me to feel this way about all of you, since I have you in my heart and, whether I am in chains or defending and confirming the gospel, all of you share in God's grace with me."
(Philippians 1:3-7)

UNITED IN PRAYER

The early Christian leader Paul was imprisoned a number of times for sharing his faith. Imagine how lonely he must have felt. Branded as an enemy of the state. Thrown into a dirty cell. Isolated from his friends. Yet, when Paul penned a letter from his jail cell to the church in Philippi, these were his words: "I thank my God every time I remember you in all my prayers for all of you, I always pray with joy. . . . It is right for me to feel this way about all of you, since I have you in my heart and, whether I am in chains or defending and confirming the gospel, all of you share in God's grace with me" (Philippians 1:3-4, 7). Alone and in trouble, somehow Paul felt neither lonely nor anxious.

How was it possible for Paul to feel such peace? Perhaps it was because he prayed for his friends and he knew that they were praying for him too. The words of Paul's letter reveal a powerful connection forged through prayer. When Christians pray for a common cause, they share an intimacy that even the worst circumstances cannot break apart. Paul was sustained, even joyous, in his persecution because he trusted in the power of Christians praying together.

We do not tend to think this way when it comes to prayer. When we think of prayer, we may imagine a solitary endeavor: a lone believer kneeling by her or his bed with folded hands. This image is true enough. Prayer is a deeply personal expression of the heart. When Jesus gave instruction in prayer, he said, "When you pray, go into your room, close the door and pray to your Father" (Matthew 6:6). Jesus did not mean that our prayer life should be a private affair, however. Our relationship with God may be deeply personal, but it was never meant to be solitary. God created us to live in community. The wonder of Paul's experience in prison is not that he was able to make it on his own but that even in that lonely place he could feel the prayers of those who loved him. Even when Christians are apart, we are united in our prayers for each other.

Paul could not have experienced such unity with his Christian friends unless they had prayed together on many occasions. Many of us feel nervous about praying with others. We do not always find it easy to invite others into such a personal experience. Yet, as many Christians since Paul have found, gathering together to pray in worship, in small groups, in partners of two, can enliven our prayer life with intimacy and power. This is the communal side of prayer. Community is where all our prayers begin.

Mark recalls:

> My first experience kneeling in prayer was with my mother beside me, helping me to say the words, "Now I lay me down to sleep." Family meals were marked by holding hands and listening to my older brother repeat his favorite blessing ("God is great, God is good..."), which he had perfected to the point that he could recite it with the pace of an auctioneer. My early prayer life included lying on a church pew, head resting in my mom's lap as I played with those tiny little offering pencils and wondered why churches and mini-golf courses required the same writing instrument. I would listen to my father's voice from his pulpit. I never followed what he said, but I had no doubt that he was speaking to God on our behalf; and I noticed that he kept using the pronoun "we." All this made me feel safe and secure—not just with my family, but with all the people surrounding me who bowed their heads before God.

Our prayers, no matter how private they may seem, embed us in the life Christians share together. Only in this soil can personal devotion flower and grow. Perhaps the primary way that Christians love one another is by praying for each other. When one is sick or suffering or confused, what do we do? We bow in prayer. As we pray for fellow believers, we cherish them in the presence of God. We encounter them, as they really are, in our communion with God. Our prayers may sometimes take place in private, but they are always deeply communal. Prayer is love, and love is always shared.

"It is only in prayer that we can communicate with one another at the deepest level of our being. Behind all words and gestures, behind all thoughts and feelings, there is an inner centre of prayer where we can meet one another in the presence of God."

Bede Griffiths

A PRAYING COMMUNITY

As a famous actress on Broadway, Helen Hayes said she spent most of her life feeling successful and self-sufficient. This changed when her daughter Mary died of polio. Hayes recalled:

> While Mary was still sick, I used to go early in the morning to a little church near the hospital to pray. There the working people came quietly to worship. I had been careless with my religion. I had rather cut God out of my life, and I didn't have the nerve at the time to ask Him to make my daughter well—I only asked Him to help me understand, to let me come in and reach Him. I prayed there every morning and I kept looking for a revelation, but nothing happened.
>
> And then, much later, I discovered that it *had* happened, right there in the church. I could recall, vividly, one by one, the people I had seen there.... Life had knocked them around, but for a brief moment they were being refreshed by an ennobling experience. It seemed as they prayed, their worn faces lighted up and became the very vessels of God. Here was my revelation. Suddenly I realized I was one of them. In my need I gained strength from the knowledge that they too had needs, I felt an interdependence with them. I experienced a flood of compassion for people. I was learning the meaning of "love thy neighbor."[1]

Praying together changes us. Yes, Helen Hayes did start with private prayer; but she did not end there. Her participation led her to see who she was in the larger context of a praying community. When we pray together, we develop an attitude of *ubuntu*. Our hearts are opened to others. We are reminded that our lives are interconnected. We see ourselves as part of something bigger than ourselves. The flame of our devotion becomes part of the warming fire of prayer.

A PEOPLE OF PRAYER

> *"[Prayer is] the basic language of the Jesus community as it is brought into being by the Spirit, and then continues to pray naturally, boldly and honestly."*
>
> *Eugene Peterson*

The early followers of Jesus were a people of prayer. The first chapter of Acts says, "They all joined together constantly in prayer" (Acts 1:14). Throughout the early centuries of Christianity, believers gathered in the morning and the evening. With the rising of the sun, they celebrated the rising of Jesus from the dead by praying together. As the sun set and day receded, they prayed for each other to remember that Jesus Christ is the true light of the world who will come again in glory. On special holy days, early Christians "kept watch" through the night with prayer vigils. No wonder that one of the titles non-Christians used for these passionate pray-ers was "those who call upon the name" of God (see Acts 9:14, 21). Praying together gave early Christians their common identity.

Community prayer was also the way the first Christians responded to important decisions and unexpected crises. When they needed a new member to join their leadership team, they prayed for wisdom. "Lord, you know everyone's heart," they prayed. "Show us which of these ... you have chosen" for this ministry (Acts 1:24). When Peter was arrested, "the church was praying to God earnestly for him" (Acts 12:5). Whenever Paul embarked on one of his many journeys, Christians gathered around him to ask God for travel mercies (Acts 21:5-6). When a little girl named Tabitha became sick and died, Peter joined others in praying for her; and she rose from the dead

(Acts 9:36-43). When a man named Publius witnessed the prayer life of the early Christians, he asked them to pray for the healing of his father (Acts 28:7-8). The early Christians were not just a people who prayed; they were a people of prayer. Everything they did was saturated with the awareness of their mutual dependence on God.

The Letter of James offers early Christians instructions about praying together: "Is anyone among you in trouble? Let them pray. Is anyone happy? Let them sing songs of praise. Is anyone among you sick? Let them call the elders of the church to pray over them and anoint them with oil in the name of the Lord. . . . Confess your sins to each other and pray for each other so that you may be healed. The prayer of a righteous person is powerful and effective" (James 5:13-16).

What is James doing here? He goads the early Christians to pray together always. Have you ever been in trouble? We all know what it is like to be in over our heads. Find another Christian, James says, and pray your way through. Are you ever happy? Of course! Then get together and offer prayers of joy and praise. Do you ever get sick? We all do. That is the time to find strength in the prayers of those who care about you. James is saying that every occasion is an opportunity to pray together and that the prayers you share will be "powerful and effective."

There are churches today that still follow the example of early Christians. Christian churches in Korea, for instance, are renowned for their passionate prayer life. Many historians trace this passion back to a powerful revival in 1907 that is known as the Korean Pentecost. This revival grew out of several prayer meetings that new Christians from Korea shared with Methodist missionaries. The fire of the Holy Spirit sparked a spiritual vitality among these early Korean congregations. Committing themselves to be a people of prayer, Korean Christians formed unique traditions modeled after the early church that continue to this day. Thousands gather at six o'clock every morning for community prayer. Twenty-four-hour prayer vigils are conducted that can last for weeks. Korean Christians offer prayers of petition in unison, a practice called *Tsong Kido*. In this practice, following a specific request, all pray aloud at the same time. Such an experience sounds like Pentecost all over again.

When an American church delegation traveled to South Korea, a member of the group offered to help the local Korean congregation. He asked again and again, "What can our congregation in the United States do for you?" Each time, he received the response, "You can pray for us." Finally, in exasperation, the American Christian said, "Now come on and tell me. We want to do something. What can we do?" Finally the Korean pastor sadly shook his head and replied, "Nothing. Nothing at all. You clearly don't believe prayer is as powerful as we do." When we trust that when Christians pray it is "powerful and effective," we truly are following the example of the first followers of Jesus.

"What we do or do not do in our communion with God now matters in some very real way for the life of the world. What we do or do not do, along with our praying neighbors, can tip a secret balance in the course of history."

John Koenig

WHAT IS INTERCESSORY PRAYER?

"To intercede is to bear others on the heart in God's presence. . . . Intercession must become not the bombardment of God with requests so much as the bringing of our desires within the streams of God's own compassion."

Michael Ramsey

Christians do not just pray with each other. We also pray for each other. When we pray on behalf of others, it is called intercessory prayer. The word *intercede* means to stand between; that is, to stand between the one prayed for and God. We may intercede for our closest loved ones and for persons we have never met. Intercessory prayer can be for the safety of one's family or for a friend who is lonely. Intercessory prayers may also be offered for the distant relative of a fellow church member or for the residents of a far-off country who are victims of a natural disaster. Intercessory prayer places God at the center of our concern for another person.

One lonely Christmas morning, a journalist named Kristin Ohlson came across a small ad in the newspaper for mass (Catholic worship) at Saint Paul's Cathedral in Cleveland. She had not been to worship since she was a child and was pretty sure she no longer believed in God. Yet, for some reason she decided to attend and was dismayed by what she discovered. She found a tiny group of aging nuns, known as the Poor Claires, who believed intercessory prayer was their one mission in life. The nuns never left the grounds of the cathedral, and each night they took turns waking at midnight to pray throughout the day for the needs of the world. Every day the nuns collected the prayer requests left in their chapel. They combed through the Cleveland papers searching for persons in crisis. Then they prayed for the needs of the world in general.

Kristin became fascinated by the commitment of these women. Eventually, she convinced them to be interviewed. After one of these conversations, Kristin experienced a touching moment with an elderly nun. The nun took Kristin's hand, kissed it, and said, "I love you." At that moment Kristin realized what prayer had given this elderly nun. "She was loving me as a fellow creature made in the image of God," Kristin wrote, when Kristin's own love was often "confined to a much thinner slice of humanity." [2]

Praying for others changes us. Prayer expands our horizons and increases our capacity to love.

"The heart that breaks open can contain the whole universe."
Johanna Rogers Macy

Our prayers may never be as pure and selfless as those of the nun Kristin Ohlson met. Yet, God still receives our prayers as heartfelt requests on behalf of others. John Mills, the founder of the North Carolina Baptist Children's Home, was visiting the orphanage late one night in 1894. He went into one of the dormitories and overheard a boy praying in the dark by his bedside: "Good Lord, we need a barrel of flour; and please send us a barrel of meal. We would thank Thee for a barrel of sugar and we need a barrel of pepper—oh hell, that's too much pepper."[3] God honors every prayer. We do not need to wait until we fully mature in our faith. The important thing is simply to begin. God will use our prayers to alter situations and over time to change us.

> *"We are not bound together by dogma or doctrine or form or denomination.... We are bound together because we are trying to learn to pray, because we are trying to learn to listen for the voice of the One Who made us and the One Who came among us and the One who will ... eventually lead us home."*
>
> *Robert Benson*

WHAT HAPPENS WHEN WE PRAY TOGETHER?

> *"More things are wrought by prayer than this world dreams of."*
>
> *Alfred, Lord Tennyson*

Mark recalls:

> When I served a small church in the mountains of North Carolina, we shared our prayer concerns each Sunday. One morning a tearful mother told about a crisis in her adult son's life that galvanized our little community in prayer. During a routine exam, a large tumor had been discovered in Scott's neck; its tentacles wrapped around many of the vitally important nerves in his neck. We gathered in prayer as

Scott traveled with his wife and parents to a famous cancer center in Houston.

The surgeon was not sure if this tumor could even be removed, but he knew he had to try. On the morning of the surgery, practically everyone in the church offered prayers for Scott. We knelt and prayed for a miracle. I was surprised when Wendell, Scott's father, called my office that morning. Actually, my heart sank. The surgery was scheduled to take many hours. I did not expect a call until late that night. Surely this was the terrible news we all feared, that the surgeon realized immediately that the tumor was impossible to remove.

Yet, Wendell said excitedly, "Mark, you won't believe this; but the surgeon said this was the simplest surgery he has ever had. Somehow the tumor shrank over the past week. He said he removed it without any problems." Our congregation gathered on Sunday to share prayers of thanksgiving.

It was a wonderful experience for our church. Yet, the prayers we offered together did not always have these results. Sometimes tumors did not shrink. Some patients we prayed for never became well.

TWO EXTREMES

What do these different results say about prayer? However we answer the question, it is probably best to avoid two extremes. On the one hand, prayer can be seen as a kind of spiritual technology with which people gain control over God and somehow direct God's bidding. Taken to its logical conclusion, this approach makes prayer an invoice that God is obliged to pay. Then, when our prayers "don't work," we blame ourselves for failing to pray in the right way.

On the other hand, prayer is sometimes seen as a kind of spiritual aerobics: an activity that may strengthen the faith of those who pray but have no effect on God. In this case, prayer is like going to the gym. Prayer works because it gives us personal benefits, making us less anxious or more sympathetic perhaps but accomplishing little beyond that. To say that prayer always changes God is to say too much. To say that prayer only changes us is to say too little.

Prayer is part of a living relationship. When we pray together, we experience communion with God and community with one another. For this reason, we may best understand prayer when we compare it to significant relationships in our lives. We do not measure the value of our relationship with a close friend or spouse by whether we always receive what we want. A good friendship or marriage is about intimacy, spending time together and sharing meaningful experiences. The same is true of prayer. Prayer is an expression of intimacy with God and other persons. Through intercessory prayer we receive the concerns, pains, and joys of another person into our hearts so that we truly share them. They become our concerns, pains, and joys. In prayer, we place them before God. Even when we do not receive the results we desire, the act of praying together opens our hearts to one another and draws us more deeply into the heart of God.

> *"Christian fellowship lives and exists by the intercession of its members for one another, or it collapses."*
>
> *Dietrich Bonhoeffer*

In her book *Two-Part Invention,* Madeleine L'Engle recalls a time she spent waiting for the results of a biopsy. "Please, dear God, don't let it be cancer," she prayed again and again. After L'Engle was diagnosed with cancer, she reflected on the value of those earlier prayers: "Prayer is love, and love is never wasted. . . . Surely the prayers have sustained me, are sustaining me. Perhaps there will be unexpected answers to these prayers, answers I may not even be aware of for years. But they are not wasted. They are not lost. I do not know where they have gone, but I believe that God holds them, hand outstretched to receive them like precious pearls."[4] Twenty years later, Madeleine L'Engle is a cancer survivor who continues to write books. During that time she has prayed often for herself and for others. Undoubtedly some of those prayers were answered as she desired, while other prayers were not. Through it all, her intimacy with those people who share her prayers and the God who receives them grows deeper.

"We must not forget that intercession is inseparable from all we are and do as Christians. It is inseparable from involvement in the pain of others, and inseparable from ... God's love in us. Intercession is ... one aspect of God's victorious assault on all that hurts and diminishes [God's] world. It is part of God's reclaiming and re-creating of all things."

Rowan Williams

PRIMING THE PUMP

Cultivating a rich prayer life takes time and practice. This may be especially true when we are learning to pray for others. Often we struggle to know whom to pray for and what needs to mention. With all the people in our lives and all the problems in the world, the task of intercessory prayer can seem daunting. But there are ways we can prime the pump of our prayer life and begin to experience the intimacy that praying for other people may bring.

One popular way to begin is to keep a prayer list. A prayer list may be composed of everyone from a few special persons in our life to thousands of people who remain unknown to us, such as people in far-off countries who are battling disease, poverty, and war. One common result of keeping a prayer list is to expand gradually the scope of our prayers. We might begin with our own needs, move to the concerns of family and friends, and then consider the needs of our church and community. Finally, we may pray for leaders of our country and the deep needs in our world. Christians have discovered all kinds of ways to maintain prayer lists. Some keep a notebook by their bed. Others keep a list on their computer so they can easily add and delete names. One member of Mark's church made her own prayer beads, each bead representing an important person in her life. However we do it, prayer lists are a great way to jog our memories about those people and situations in need and to keep us returning to God in prayer.

Another way to cultivate a rich prayer life is to find a prayer partner who promises to meet with you at regular times to pray for those in need. In Andy's congregation there is the Healing Shawl Ministry. A group of women gather one day a month to knit shawls and blankets for persons in need. These knitted articles are presented to children at their baptism, to people who grieve, to folks in the hospital, and to older persons who are homebound. As the women begin to knit, they offer a prayer for the people for whom they are knitting. The women visit as they knit, sharing with one another how they have felt God's healing power in their own lives—recovering from divorce, surviving cancer, overcoming grief. When they finish knitting, the women pray over the shawl or blanket that the person who receives it will also feel God's power.

KNOWING HOW TO PRAY FOR OTHERS

When we struggle to know what to pray, we can always turn to Scripture for guidance. Quickly skimming Acts and the letters of the New Testament can give us a sense of the circumstances that inspired early Christians to pray. For instance, the first followers of Jesus Christ often prayed for the spiritual maturity of other Christians (Ephesians 1:15-18; Philippians 1:9-11; Colossians 1:9-10). We find this model in Paul's letter to the Galatians: "My dear children, for whom I am again in the pains of childbirth until Christ is formed in you" (Galatians 4:19). Early Christians prayed that those who were sick would receive healing (Acts 9:36-42; 28:7-8; James 5:13-16) and that those wrongly imprisoned might be released (Acts 12:5-12). Early Christians also prayed for persons outside the Christian movement, including civil authorities (1 Timothy 2:1-2). Following this example, we might divide our prayers into categories, praying that those we love will grow in grace; that those who are sick, suffering, or imprisoned might find relief; and that political leaders may be open to the guidance of God.

Perhaps the simplest prayer strategy comes from the Bible. We can return to the example of Paul and the letter he wrote to the Philippians while he was in jail: "I thank my God every time I remember you" (Philippians 1:3). Whenever someone comes to mind, someone you know very well or very little, just offer a little prayer of thanksgiving and remembrance.

There is no right or wrong way to pray for others. Prayer is heart language. Follow the rhythms of your body. If you are alert and imaginative in the morning, try getting up a bit earlier to remember others in prayer. If you are a night owl, offer your prayers when you are up alone and the house is quiet. You can pray for others when folding the laundry, walking your dog, or commuting to work. The possibilities for prayer, the opportunities to commune with God and be in community with others, are endless. The fire of prayer will draw us around the hearth of God's love.

The following is an ancient Christian prayer, "Veni Creator," that emerged out of the heartfelt yearning of early Christians:

Come, Holy Spirit
and send out a ray
of your heavenly light. . . .

O blessed light,
fill the innermost hearts
of those who believe in you. . . .

Wash what is unclean,
water what is arid,
heal what is wounded.

Bend what is stiff,
warm what is cold,
guide what has gone astray.[5]

Unknown author, ninth century

---

1. From "This I Believe, " by Helen Hayes, on National Public Radio September 26, 2005 (www.npr.org).

2. From *Stalking the Divine*, by Kristin Ohlson (Plume, 2004).

3. From *Tough Mercy,* by Ted Chandler (Baptist Children's Homes, 1990); pages 49–50.

4. From *Two-Part Invention,* by Madeleine L'Engle (Harper and Row, 1988); pages 186–87.

5. From *Watch and Pray: Christian Teachings on the Practice of Prayer,* edited by Lorraine Kisly (Bell Tower, 2002); page 80.

Five:
What's the Deal With Miracles?

Signs and Wonders

"There are only two ways to live your life. One is as though nothing is a miracle. The other is as if everything is."
Albert Einstein

"Everyone was filled with awe, and many wonders and miracles were accomplished."
(Acts 2:43, authors' paraphrase)

"In Lystra there sat a man who was lame. He had been that way from birth and had never walked. He listened to Paul as he was speaking. Paul looked directly at him, saw that he had faith to be healed and called out, 'Stand up on your feet!' At that, the man jumped up and began to walk. When the crowd saw what Paul had done, they shouted.... 'The gods have come down to us in human form!' Barnabas they called Zeus, and Paul they called Hermes because he was the chief speaker. The priest of Zeus, whose temple was just outside the city, brought bulls and wreaths to the city gates because he and the crowd wanted to offer sacrifices to them [Barnabas and Paul]. But when the apostles Barnabas and Paul heard of this, they tore their clothes and rushed out into the crowd, shouting: 'Friends, why are you doing this? We too are only human, like you. We are bringing you good news, telling you to turn from these worthless things to the living God, who made heaven and earth and sea and everything in them.' "

(Acts 14:8-15)

Many of us believe that God performs miracles every day. Yet, there is some tension in this belief because miracles do not seem to happen as they once did. Once upon a time miracles were, well, miraculous. They were glorious, earth-shaking events so remarkable that they fill us with wonder to this day. God parting the Red Sea. Jesus calming a storm. Peter bringing a little girl named Tabitha back to life. In biblical times, God changed circumstances in remarkable ways. We believe that God is still at work in the world, but things seem different today. How do we make sense of this apparent change? Does God work differently now? Or has our perspective changed?

We can begin to respond to these questions by considering a miracle reported in the Book of Acts. When Paul and Barnabas arrived in the Roman city of Lystra, they encountered a man who had been handicapped since his birth (Acts 14:8-18). He was unable to walk. Paul looked directly at the man and said, "Stand up!" When the man immediately jumped to his feet, the people of Lystra were so amazed that they jumped to all the wrong conclusions. Priests showed up with two large oxen ready to make a sacrifice to Paul and Barnabas. These two early church leaders were about to be declared gods by popular demand!

Paul and Barnabas quickly recognized where the crowd had become confused. The crowd had focused their attention on the miracle itself—the "special effect"—that left them in amazement. Paul and Barnabas had a different perspective. They focused on the living God who is behind all the miracles of life. Paul cried, "Friends, why are you doing this?... Turn from these worthless things to the living God, who made heaven and earth and sea and everything in them" (Acts 14:15). Paul urged them to focus their attention on God who "has shown kindness by giving you rain from heaven and crops in their seasons," the same God who "fills your hearts with joy" (Acts 14:17). Paul proclaimed that the miraculous is all around us. Even things that we take for granted, such as food and water and simple pleasures, are all evidence of God's love. We do not have to wait for the spectacular to sense God's presence. God is already at work everywhere we look.

CLOSING OUR EYES

> *"I think the people to feel saddest for are people . . . who lost or became numb to the sensation of wonder—people who closed the doors that lead us into the secret world—or who had the doors closed for them by time and neglect."*
>
> *Douglas Coupland*

The problem is that our way of seeing has changed. Compared with people in ancient times, we are much less likely to notice God at work in our world. Two modern forces have contributed to our limited awareness when it comes to miracles. One of these forces is materialism, which assumes that natural, material things are more reliable indicators of reality than supernatural or spiritual ones. At a basic level, materialism is just sound common sense. We can reach out and touch material things. We can hold them in our hands. We can measure them and study them by breaking them apart into manageable pieces. We just cannot do that with spiritual things, such as love or the presence of God. Those phenomena are hard to measure and impossible to prove in scientific terms.

Materialism has helped us in many ways. For instance, the advances of modern medicine rely upon the assumption that people get sick, not because they "made the gods angry," but because of anomalies in the natural world. Materialism has brought many good things; but when it is carried too far, it makes us unduly suspicious of what we cannot explain. Reality becomes limited to what we can see and hear, what we can touch and taste. Our perspective becomes narrowed. Our vision is reduced to the visible world that we can break apart and analyze. According to Louis Patrick, the familiar children's song "Twinkle, Twinkle, Little Star" should be given new lyrics:

> Twinkle, twinkle, little star.
> I do not need to wonder what you are.
> You're just so much combusting mass
> Of C and N and hydrogen gas![1]

Another force contributing to our limited awareness of miracles is cynicism. Cynicism comes about when we place our hopes in the possibility of miracles but then become disillusioned. In the 1992 movie *Leap of Faith,* Steve Martin plays the role of Jonas Nightingale, a high-tech faith healer who squeezes money out of people by convincing them that a miracle is just a touch away. He claims to have a magic touch, and of course he stages every bit of it. At each stop on his tour Jonas cons people out of their money and leaves them disappointed. He convinces himself that even though he cannot provide any real hope, he at least offers the crowds a good show. When Jonas' tour bus breaks down in rural Kansas and he falls in love with a local waitress who has a brother with a handicapping condition, he begins to wish that miracles were possible. Unfortunately, Jonas has become much too cynical to believe that.

The problem with both materialism and cynicism is that they reduce our capacity for wonder. When we are children, the world is full of wondrous things; but gradually our sense of wonder wanes. As we grow older, we understand more and more of the world around us. If we are not careful, our increased understanding has a negative effect on us. We may become overconfident of our ability to explain and too quickly cast doubt on the inexplicable. When this happens, our experience of God's world becomes flat and narrow. We start to miss the remarkable things happening all around us.

The poet Elizabeth Barrett Browning once poked fun at such a limited perspective. Referring to the Old Testament story of the burning bush, she wrote,

> The earth is ablaze with the fire of God,
> but only those who see it take their shoes off;
> the rest sit around and pick blackberries![2]

Like the people of Lystra described in the passage of Scripture at the beginning of this chapter, we think that a miracle must be some glorious flash of divine power. Miracles are all around us, however. The fact that we do not acknowledge them does not mean they are not there. Most miracles happen quietly, barely noticed by the majority of people.

BECOMING AMPHIBIOUS

"We are alive within mystery, by miracle."
Wendell Berry

As people of faith, we must never forget that there is a spiritual force enlivening every material occurrence. When we open our eyes to the possibility of miracles, we begin to see "ordinary" occurrences as signs of something more. A sunset at the beach. An elderly couple holding hands in the park. The selfless act of a friend. Recognizing these occurrences for what they are, we may slowly begin to trust that God is at work in the world and in our lives. Like a frog that can adapt to life in the water or on dry land, we become spiritually amphibious. We live with both feet planted in the "real world" but also hold out the possibility of something more, a world of mystery and miracle that enlivens our material world with God's mercy and grace. As we become amphibious, we recognize that there are things we simply cannot explain or understand; and the thought of that possibility fills us with wonder.

"Miracles . . . seem to me to rest not so much upon faces or voices or healing power coming suddenly near to us from afar off, but upon our perceptions being made finer, so that for a moment our eyes can see and our ears can hear what is there about us always."

Willa Cather

Consider this modern miracle story reported on the National Public Radio program "All Things Considered." In April 1998, a series of tornadoes ripped through the southeastern United States. One of the places destroyed was a church building in Alabama. When the tornado hit, the children's choir had been rehearsing in the choir room. The pastor saw the tornado coming. He quickly gathered all the children into the church's main hallway, where they huddled together while mighty winds tore their church apart. In an effort to calm the children's fear, the pastor led them in singing "Jesus Loves the Little Children." Although some of the children were hurt, amazingly no one was killed.

The most penetrating part of the broadcast was the report of a little girl who said, "While we were singing, I saw the angels holding up the hallway. But the winds were so strong that the angels shouted out, 'We need help!' So some more angels came and helped them."[3]

What can we do with such a report? We may or may not choose to take it at face value. But if we are spiritually amphibious, we probably will not reject it automatically. We recognize that no matter what role we decide to give to a little girl's imagination, something wonderful happened that day. The story, whatever we make of it, becomes a testament to God's love and care and a window to a deeper mystery.

SIGNS AND WONDERS

" 'Miracle' is simply the wonder of the unique that points us back to the wonder of the everyday."

Maurice Friedman

In biblical language, miraculous events would be called signs and wonders. Because we are most accustomed to thinking of miracles as wonders, let us consider that definition first. A wonder is an unexpected event that we find extraordinary. We can see this in the popular use of the word *miracle.* When the New York Mets won the 1969 World Series, they were dubbed "the Miracle Mets." When the United States men's hockey team upset the seemingly invincible Soviet Union team in the 1980 Olympics, the game was called "the Miracle on Ice." Late night infomercials tout weight loss treatments as "miracle pills," while advertisements for cosmetic surgery espouse "the wonders of botox." All these refer in some way to extraordinary, unexpected events.

Yet, when Christians speak of miracles, we are more specific than this. An underrated team winning a championship might be extraordinary, but it is not what Christians call a miracle. A miracle is a wonder that comes from God. Miracles are special acts of God in the world. From our human perspective, miracles are supernatural. They are beyond the regular, consistent pattern of natural occurrences. A miracle happens when God briefly disrupts the ordinary patterns of nature for a specific purpose. This means that miracles are different from the examples above. They are more than just unusual. They are more than remarkable. Miracles are gifts from God.

The Christian author C. S. Lewis once described miracles as God's signature. "I contend," Lewis wrote, "that in all miracles … God does suddenly and locally something that God has done or will do in general. Each miracle writes for us in small letters something that God has always written, or will write, in letters almost too large to be noticed, across the whole canvas of Nature.… Each carries the signature of the God we know … from Nature"[4]

As wonders, miracles bestow on us the gift of mystery. When life moves along in expected, routine ways, we can become lulled into a spiritual sleep in which we come to expect no surprises. Miracles are wonders in that they awaken our senses to the things of God. Mark recalls:

> When I walk my dogs, I enjoy watching them sniff at every bush and tree. For them, everything has a hidden olfactory significance of which I am unaware. The wonderful thing about miracles is that they make us aware of the things of God that are all around us. Once you see a wonder and recognize that it is of God, then you are caught forever with God's presence at the center of all things. The world becomes alive in a new way that devours the ordinary and the mundane.

Miracles, in addition to being wonders, are also signs. This designation means that God's wonders are not mere spectacles, with no purpose other than to amaze. When Jesus performed miracles, he was not resorting to magic tricks in order to prove his power and dazzle the crowds. Jesus did not feed five thousand persons just to show off! Authentic miracles communicate. They signal God's presence among us. When Jesus performed miracles, he often spoke of the kingdom of heaven. A miracle is a sign, clear evidence of God's presence and power. When God performs a miracle, we must recognize that we have special meaning to God. Each time God acts in this special way, we see that we are important to God.

> *"A miracle is not a stained-glass window to look at, but a transparent window to look through."*
>
> *Jaroslav Pelikan*

Emily Weichman suffered a stroke as a small child. She remained a weak youngster, never enjoying a robust state of health. In September 1991, the Weichmans were driving across Wyoming. They were in a mostly deserted area when Emily said, "Mommy, I'm sick!" Soon thereafter, she began to vomit. The Weichmans suddenly knew the grip of fear. They realized Emily must be taken to a hospital immediately. But how? They were in an isolated, deserted place with no idea of how to find a hospital.

Then something mysterious happened. Everyone in the van began to see blue signs with a large white *H*—the well-known marker designating a hospital. They followed the signs for quite a distance. Finally they were led to a hospital. Emily's condition was quickly diagnosed, and her life was spared.

Once Emily was in her hospital room, Mrs. Weichman told the doctor, "If it weren't for those hospital signs, we might still be driving around." The physician was puzzled. "What signs?" "The ones lining our route," the mother explained. "They were literally a lifesaver—we couldn't have found the hospital without them." The confused doctor responded, "I live about eight miles out on that road. I travel it every day here, and I've never seen any hospital signs."

The next day Mrs. Weichman phoned the Rock Springs Chamber of Commerce to ask about the signs. "There have never been any hospital signs along that route," said a city official.

Emily is now healthy and happy. Her parents consider her a miracle child.[5]

In Emily's case, it appeared that God literally used signs to perform a miracle. Generally speaking, though, all miracles are signs. They direct us beyond our ordinary routines and assumptions, pointing the way to the mystery of God's love at the heart of it all.

A sign from God does not have to be earthshaking. It can be a small, quiet moment that leads us to reflect on God's mercy and grace. Mark recalls a seemingly small event at his church that changed the way he looked at the world:

> One day, I was walking through the gathering space in our church when a member motioned for me to come over. I found her, hands on her knees, bent over and staring at the base of the wall. We shook our heads in disbelief. Soon others gathered around us, all looking down at the same spot. Before us was a tiny flower that had somehow pushed through all those layers of concrete to blossom. I had never seen a flower growing out of the brick wall before. The funny thing is, the flower had been there for weeks. I must have walked by it hundreds of times, but I never noticed it. Yet, once I saw it, I could not pass

> by without pausing to look and to smile. It became for me an expression of how tenacious God's love is, struggling to break through all the walls in my heart. That little flower became something more than an unlikely occurrence. It became a sign of God's gracious presence. To this day, the memory of that flower makes me reflect and wonder.

MIRACLES AND CHRISTIAN COMMUNITY

Perhaps the most wonderful part of seeing that flower in the wall was sharing the experience with others. This community experience is consistent with the testimony of the first followers of Jesus Christ. The people of God take part as a group in God's miracles. The Christian community is the medium for God's miraculous work. This is the promise God makes at the beginning of the Book of Acts: "You will receive power when the Holy Spirit comes on you; and you will be my witnesses … to the ends of the earth" (Acts 1:8). Miracles are not meant to be private experiences. Miracles are signs to be interpreted together. They are wonders to be shared.

Through the eyes of the community, we begin to experience miraculous signs and wonders in ways that we surely would have missed before. Mark recalls:

> Shortly after moving to a new congregation, I attended a Sunday school class party. I was surprised when out of the blue a man took out a violin and started to play. When he had finished, everyone broke out into thunderous applause. Ladies wept. Men slapped him on the back with congratulations. You would have thought it was a Izhak Perlman concert. It was not. It actually sounded as if he were rubbing two cats together. You see, the man had recently lost his wife after many years of marriage. He had taken up the violin just six months before as a way to assuage his grief. The miracle was not the event itself but the way his gift was received by a community who cared. Whatever sounds he made, they actually heard something beautiful.

James Howell recalls, "A few years ago a friend of mine spent a week at Lourdes—the shrine in France where the Virgin Mary appeared to fourteen-year-old Bernadette Soubirous in 1858. Thousands of gallons of water flow from a spring there each day, and thousands have claimed to have been cured in its streams. When my friend returned, I asked her, 'Did you see any miracles?' She said, 'Oh yes, every day.' 'Every day? Tell me.' She explained, 'Every day at Lourdes, no matter who you are, or where you are from, or what's wrong with you, you are welcomed and loved.' "[6]

"Where there is great love there are always miracles."
Willa Cather

REDISCOVERING WONDER

"I have spent my life watching, not to see beyond the world, merely to see, great mystery, what is plainly before my eyes. . . . With all respect to heaven, the scene of miracles is here, among us."
Marilynne Robinson

We need the Christian community to help us see with new eyes. If we continue to view the world with materialist and cynical eyes, our focus will be limited to the horizon of our understanding. We will, as Paul reminded the people of Lystra, miss the signs and wonders of God that are all around us. Andy recalls:

> One day, I woke up to a cold, hard rain. I had left my umbrella in my office and knew that my day was off to a bad start. As I drove to my church, I dreaded getting wet as I ran from my car to the building. The large, hard drops of rain beat against my car and then attacked me as I got out of the car. As I ran up to the door, a large glass door with plate-glass windows to each side, I saw one of our church preschool children watching me. She was simply standing at the window watching the rain. When I entered, I turned and said to her, "What do you think about this rain?" I expected her to say that it was wet or cold or nasty. Instead, she replied, "Isn't it beautiful!"

> Kneeling beside her, I looked again at the rain. She was right. It was beautiful! I saw large falling drops, dancing puddles, and moisture reviving the earth.

The greatest miracles—the birth of Christ, the rebirth of a new Christian—happen quietly. They are barely noticed by the majority of people. We need others around us to help us see these events for what they truly are.

As we acknowledge the possibility of mystery and miracles, we find a way of life beyond materialism and cynicism. We discover healing and hope. The writer Elizabeth Gray Vining was once suffering a debilitating grief. Her heart felt frozen. Her life was without hope. One morning she woke to hear what sounded like rain on the roof of her porch. As she rubbed her eyes at the window, she was surprised to see the sun streaming in. The patter was not rain but thousands of locust blossoms falling all around her home and covering the roof. She wrote that at that moment the ice in her soul began to break apart. Vining detected God's presence in the blossoms. If she had not taken a leap of faith, the flowers might have seemed a pointless coincidence; and she would have remained locked in her grief.

Until we rediscover wonder, we are trapped by the limited horizons of our own understanding. God wants more for us.

We opened this chapter with a quote from Albert Einstein. This genius, who was able to solve some of the most perplexing problems in physics, did not let his understanding limit his ability to experience wonder. To a generation bound by materialism and cynicism, Einstein said, "Come let us see that the universe is mysterious."[6] This same invitation is offered to everyone who shares in Christian community. We are invited to gather around the fire of awe. There, we learn to expand our horizons. We read the signs and experience the wonder of God's love.

---

1. From "The 'Ah' of Wonder," by Louis Patrick, in *Sermons From Duke Chapel,* edited by Will Willimon (Duke University Press, 2005); page 237.

2. From "Aurora Leigh," by Elizabeth Barrett Browning.

3. From "All Things Considered: Morning Edition," April 13, 1998 (National Public Radio).

4. From *Miracles,* by C. S. Lewis (Macmillan, 1947); page 140.

5. From *Miracles and Wonders: How God Changes His Natural Laws to Benefit You,* by Calvin Miller (WarnerFaith, 2003); pages 158–59.

6. From *Yours Are the Hands of Christ,* by James Howell (Upper Room, 1998); page 67.

7. From *Miracles and Wonders: How God Changes His Natural Laws to Benefit You,* by Calvin Miller; page 102.

Six:
What Do We Have in Common?

Stewardship

"Love consists in sharing what one has and what one is with those one loves."

Ignatius of Loyola

"All who believed lived in close fellowship and possessed all things in common. They sold their belongings and property and gave their money to anyone who had need."

(Acts 2:44-45, authors' paraphrase)

"I thought it necessary to urge the brothers to visit you in advance, and finish the arrangements for the generous gift that you had promised. Then it will be ready as a generous gift, not as one grudgingly given. Remember this: Whoever sows sparingly will also reap sparingly, and whoever sows generously will also reap generously."

(2 Corinthians 9:5-6)

POSSESSIVENESS

In the movie *Two Weeks Notice,* Hugh Grant plays George Wade, a spoiled corporate magnate who is obsessed with money and possessions. Proving that opposites attract, George falls for Lucy Kelson, a do-gooding lawyer who spends her days trying to save a dilapidated but deeply cherished community center. When Lucy's mother discovers that George is behind a plan to tear down the community center and replace it with a corporate office building, she confronts him: "Are you going to reconsider putting up that building?" "I'm afraid that's impossible," explains George. "We stand to make fifty million dollars." Mrs. Kelson retorts, "Fifty million dollars! I think that it's obscene to have that much wealth! How can you sleep at night?" Unflustered, George deadpans, "Well, I have a machine beside my bed that simulates the sound of the ocean."[1]

Poor George is clueless. He sees his life in terms of his possessions—from his corporate office building to the specially designed sleep machine by his bed. Placing a higher value on what he owns than on what he owes to others, George fails to recognize the things in life that bring true fulfillment.

According to author James Kuntsler, George is not alone. In Kuntsler's book *The Geography of Nowhere,* he observes that over the last sixty years Americans have "mutated from citizens to consumers." Citizens feel an obligation "to care about their fellow citizens," whereas consumers see themselves and others from a very different perspective. "The trouble with being consumers," writes Kuntsler, "is that consumers have no duties or responsibilities or obligations to their fellow consumers."[2]

"Something we were withholding made us weak
Until we found it was ourselves."
Robert Frost

In our culture, consuming is touted as the path to the good life. Television commercials and clever "product placements" in movies tempt us with the latest model and the newest product. Huge billboards and tiny Internet pop-up ads bombard us with information about all the stuff we do not yet own. When this activity becomes a way of life, we do not just consume things; we become consumers.

We begin to define ourselves by what we own, and we devote ourselves to acquiring more—more money, more stuff, and more entertaining experiences. We gradually come to see every part of life in terms of personal ownership. You can hear it in the way we speak. A person is said to "possess" talent or to "have" friends. These days we speak less about sharing a life and more about "acquiring a lifestyle." All these expressions suggest that we have come to see ourselves not as persons living in community, but as consumers striving to possess all that we possibly can.

> *"We break our hearts, all of us, trying to keep things that do not belong to us."*
>
> *Myrtle Reed*

Mark recalls:

> Driving home from my twentieth high school reunion, it occurred to me how my high school buddies and I related to each other that evening much as we did twenty years earlier. Without making it obvious, we checked out who drove the most luxurious car, who had the sharpest clothes, who had the most exciting job, and who lived in the most interesting place. Reflecting on our conversations, I detected the old pecking order that had characterized our friendships long ago.
>
> Twenty years later we still were not all that interested in each other's lives. We did not ask about each other's values, convictions, or relationships; we focused instead on the variety of possessions we owned. Standing around the punch bowl that evening, we learned more about our stuff than about our souls, more about our tastes than about our passions, more about our lifestyles than about our lives.

This kind of experience is characteristic of our age. Perhaps it is inevitable when most of us see the world through the eyes of a consumer. When we fall into that trap, we start making all the wrong assumptions. We assume that all we possess belongs to us and no one else and that what we do with possessions is our business and no one else's. This perspective is very different from the Christian vision of life. Christians believe that all the things we think we own are really gifts from God. We hold them in sacred trust, and we use them for the common good. God is not impressed by what we possess but by how we share. We are called to live, not as individual consumers, but as members of the family of God, freely sharing our possessions and our lives.

EARLY CHRISTIANS AS MODELS OF SHARING

"Passage after passage [in the Book of Acts] admonishes those who would follow the Way that they must sell all they have and disperse the money to the poor, thereby buying for themselves a place in the Kingdom of God. These are not easy instructions to follow, but ... they became—and have remained for us as—the Christian ideal."

Phyllis A. Tickle

The first followers of Jesus saw their life together from the perspective of trusted relationships. Shortly after Pentecost, they displayed a dramatic expression of mutual care: "All the believers were together and had everything in common. They sold property and possessions to give to anyone who had need" (Acts 2:44-45). When some of their members were suffering hardships, the community's response was straightforward. They shared. They shared their possessions. They shared their lives. Their generosity inspired a common vision, as the Book of Acts later proclaims, "one in heart and mind" (Acts 4:32). The early Christians were no longer solitary individuals but a transformed community willing to share all things in common. They became the family of God.

In later years, Christian acts of sharing became more organized. Storehouses of donated money and food were created to care for the sick and the poor. By AD 250, the Christian community in Rome supported 1500 needy persons with this method. In the fourth century, a Christian leader named Basil built a huge storehouse just outside the city gates of Caesarea, where a treasury of money collected from wealthy Christians was kept and put to use whenever Christians of the city were in need.

These expressions of generosity were not a form of communism. The first Christians did not abolish private property. They were not required to sell everything they owned. Yet, whenever there was a need, they found a way to help. They refused to place individual property rights or personal desires above their commitment to each other. Sharing their possessions was not a requirement for living in community but rather a free expression of love and concern.

THE JERUSALEM COLLECTION

Around AD 50, the region around Jerusalem was hit with a terrible famine. Poor people from surrounding villages poured into the city looking for work. Many joined the Christian community there. This community of people who had cared so faithfully for their own now needed help. So Paul began the first world-relief program in the history of the church, called the Jerusalem Collection.

As part of the Jerusalem Collection, Paul raised money from the churches in Macedonia, Galatia, and Ephesus. When the church in Corinth was reluctant to help, Paul explained that Christians share their possessions and their lives—not out of obligation, but as an expression of gratitude for the grace God had offered them. In the process of explaining, Paul discussed the ideal of Christian sharing in ways that are still helpful to us today.

The Corinthians were not selfish people. They had been affected by the famine too and felt that the resources they had left were not sufficient to help. To encourage them, Paul described how the grace of God works in our lives. He told them how the churches in

Macedonia, poor as they were, had responded to God's grace in their lives by giving even beyond their ability. "In the midst of a very severe trial," Paul wrote, "their overflowing joy . . . welled up in rich generosity" (2 Corinthians 8:2). Paul reminded the Corinthians that all Christians enjoy the eternal benefit of Christ's riches; that is, regardless of how limited our material resources may be, we are wealthy in the things that really matter (2 Corinthians 6:10). Later Paul spelled this out clearly: "Whoever sows sparingly will also reap sparingly, and whoever sows generously will also reap generously" (2 Corinthians 9:6).

Paul went on to tell the Corinthians that even when resources seem scarce, we can share out of the abundance of God's grace. When we do this, we pass God's generosity on to others; and a miracle occurs. A new kind of equality springs up between us. Paul expressed it this way: "Our desire is not that others might be relieved while you are hard pressed, but that there might be equality. At the present time your plenty will supply what they need, so that in turn their plenty will supply what you need" (2 Corinthians 8:13-14). By taking part in the Jerusalem Collection, the Corinthians would be sharing their spiritual gifts. They would have the opportunity to worship together as one family of God. There would be a spiritual unity that would not have been possible before.

"It's not what you gather, but what you scatter that tells what kind of life you have lived."

Helen Walton

A COMMUNITY OF GRACE

In the first chapter of this book, we wrote that each one of us longs for true community and that buried within that yearning is a longing for God. God responds to our deepest yearnings. The theological name for God's response is "grace." At its most basic level, grace is simply the loving presence of God. Grace is the gift of God's own self. There is no greater expression of that gift than Jesus Christ. We sense this in an ancient title for Christ, *Emmanuel,* which means "God is with us." In Jesus Christ, God shares our lives in the most radical way possible. God becomes human and lives among us!

According to the Book of Acts, grace extends beyond the earthly life of Jesus. God's presence does not end when the risen Christ ascends into heaven. God's own Spirit is poured out at Pentecost, signaling a new way that God is present among us. We encounter God not only in Christ but also in each other. "If anyone is in Christ, the new creation has come: The old has gone, the new is here!... We are therefore Christ's ambassadors, as though God were making his appeal through us" (2 Corinthians 5:17, 20). We are called to live together in a way that makes God's love visible to others. Through worship and prayer, baptism and Communion, we experience the "means of grace" that open our lives to one another and to God. Grace flows in and through us like blood flowing through the arteries of a human body. Our new reality in Christ is a community of grace.

How do we live into this new reality? First, we leave behind the consumer perspective and dare to become dis-possessed. No longer tied to our possessions, we see them as blessings from God and allow them to flow freely through our lives to others. Next, we acknowledge that following Christ is not just about sharing our things but also about sharing our selves. We freely extend to others our time, talents, gifts, and service. Finally, we discover the joy of mutual sharing. We begin to see our lives from a new perspective, leaving behind the individualism of consumers for the intimacy and openness of Christian community. When we experience this, we learn not only how to give of our possessions and ourselves but also how to receive freely what others have to share with us.

SHARING OUR POSSESSIONS

"I place no value on anything I possess, except in relationship to the kingdom of God."

David Livingston

Consumers seek security in the things they own. They become attached to them. The word *attachment* comes from ancient roots meaning "staked" or "nailed to." This suggests that sometimes what makes us feel secure may also limit us. If we stay at home each evening glued to the shopping channels on television or spend every Saturday wandering aimlessly through the mall, we will not experience the kind of relationships God created us to have. Our hearts will remain tethered to something other than the love of God and others.

This does not mean that it is wrong to enjoy our possessions. It simply means that possessions are mixed blessings. We must handle them with care. Depending on how we use them, possessions either add to our lives or deplete our souls. If we cling to our possessions as sources of security or personal power, they will make us miserable. Our possessions will distract us from the life God created us to live. Yet, if we see possessions as blessings to be received with gratitude and shared in joy, we will enjoy them more than ever.

An ancient Christian leader from Africa named Aurelius Augustine recognized the truth of that statement. Augustine said that when we find ourselves clinging to our possessions, we are simply making too much of them. We are treating them as our heart's desire. This behavior is harmful to us, not because possessions are evil, but because God is the true object of our desire. We were created to seek God for our security and then to enjoy everything God gives us as blessings. For Augustine, the question is not about what we own but about what owns us. If all our attention is spent acquiring, using, and protecting our possessions, there is little time and energy left to cultivate a relationship with God.

In the Bible we read that people who are baptized into Christian community enter a new reality where they are "liberated from … bondage" and "brought into the freedom and glory of the children of God" (Romans 8:21). Part of this freedom is relief from being bound to our possessions. This is the freedom that the early Christians of Macedonia experienced. They gave to the church in Jerusalem not just according to their means, but beyond those means. How could they dare to do this? They shared without caution because they knew that possessions do not last. Neither does wealth. Only grace, as Paul said, is eternal. When we realize this, we see our possessions in their true light. They are temporary blessings that are meant to be shared. When we dare to release what God has given us, we act as trustees. We freely distribute what has been given to us, and we trust the vast resources of divine grace to supply all our needs. We learn to ask different questions, not "How much of what I own can I afford to share?" but "In light of what I have been given and who I am called to be, how much of what I possess can I afford to keep?"

> *"We believe God is the owner of all things and that the individual holding of property is … a sacred trust under God. Private property is to be used for the manifestation of Christian love …. to support the Church's mission in the world."*
>
> *The Articles of Religion XV*

Elisha, a member of Mark's congregation, told him about a fisherman she had encountered while vacationing on the tiny Greek island of Kea. Every morning Elisha enjoyed watching the lone fisherman as he lowered his net from a small, rickety boat; waited patiently; and then pulled in his catch. Each afternoon she watched again as he rolled in his nets and returned to shore. There a long line of friends greeted him. They cheered and hugged the fisherman while holding out empty baskets. The fisherman smiled as he filled each of their baskets with fish.

After witnessing this routine for several days, Elisha finally could not contain her curiosity. She asked, "Why do you give away so many of your fish?" The fisherman just smiled at her and shook his head. Elisha persisted, offering what she believed to be a helpful lesson in small-business economics. "If you took all the fish you caught to the market and sold them, you could purchase a new boat. Eventually you could save enough money to hire an employee. With him you could catch even more fish, and one day you might have enough money to buy more boats and hire more men. Don't you see the tremendous opportunity you are missing by giving away so many fish?"

When the fisherman heard this, the smile disappeared from his face. He said crossly, "Stupid American! I follow your plan so I can do what? Have a new boat and a hired man? What if everything you say is true? Still at the end of the day, I will have the same fish for dinner that I have always had. And with your plan, I will not get to laugh and eat with the friends who meet me each day at the shore."

Throughout the rest of her vacation, Elisha reflected on the fisherman's response. She realized that while she knew how to make a profit, the Greek fisherman knew how to add value to his life. When she returned home, the memory of the fisherman inspired her to volunteer as a counselor in her church. She continues to teach families in financial trouble how to add value to their lives by learning to consume less so that they may have more to save and to give.

SHARING OUR SELVES

In the sixteenth century, a Spanish soldier named Ignatius of Loyola felt called by God to start a Christian community. Those who joined his "Society of Jesus" (also known as the Jesuits) not only vowed to share all their worldly possessions but also to make extreme personal sacrifices. They promised, for instance, to go anywhere in the world in order to teach others what it means to follow Jesus. Perhaps Ignatius was reflecting on such selfless acts of generosity when he said that genuinely loving others requires more than sharing our material possessions with them; it requires sharing who we are.

The Jesuits discovered what the earliest Christians also knew: To follow Jesus is to learn to give ourselves on behalf of others. As the Book of Acts puts it, "All the believers were together and had everything in common" (Acts 2:44). The believers did not just share possessions or wealth; they offered to one another the gift of themselves. When another Christian was sick, they provided care. When another was lonely, they gave attention. With each and every one, they shared love. This is the true attitude of *ubuntu*. It consists, as Ignatius might put it today, not just of opening our wallets, but of opening our lives to one another.

A Christian writer named Henri Nouwen spent much of his career teaching at Harvard University. While he was there, he became known for his unusual generosity, sharing from his possessions and of himself. Although books were precious to him, Nouwen gave thousands away to anyone who asked. If he heard that a friend on the other side of the country was sick, Nouwen would not hesitate to catch the next plane for a visit. Once when Nouwen was traveling in Mexico, a friend picked him up at the Cuernevaca airport. The friend immediately noticed that Nouwen had nothing with him except the clothes on his back. Later, the friend learned that Nouwen had encountered someone in need before leaving Cuernevaca and had given that person all his clothes, his money, and everything he had with him.[3]

Years later, Henri Nouwen received God's call in his life to give of himself in a more fundamental way. He left Harvard to join a Christian community in Toronto called Daybreak. He lived there for years, tending to every need of a person with severe mental and physical handicaps. In the process, he learned to give not only his possessions, but his time, his attention, and his nearly constant care. In his diary Nouwen expressed his gratitude for discovering "a community of people who could lead me closer to the heart of God." Describing his joy, he wrote that "it felt like coming home."[4]

"A man there was, though some did count him mad,
The more he cast away the more he had."
John Bunyan

A SHARED LIFE

From some of our earliest experiences as Christians, we learn that giving is a combination of sharing our possessions and ourselves. Receiving a quarter from your father to drop in the collection plate at church or to give to a homeless person, accompanying your mother to a grieving neighbor's house with a plate of food, helping your brother trim the lawn of an elderly neighbor—these experiences teach us more than generosity; they are experiments in Christian community and the beginnings of a shift in perspective from "me" to "we." The culmination of this shift occurs as we move beyond sharing part of ourselves with others to enter a new reality in which all of life is shared together as the body of Christ.

Paul understood that in the body of Christ, every single organism is intimately connected. "The eye cannot say to the hand, 'I don't need you!' And the head cannot say to the feet, 'I don't need you!' " (1 Corinthians 12:21). When one suffers, all are weakened. When one rejoices, all grow stronger. As followers of Jesus, we share a common bond and a joint mission. Together we support each other and carry the love of Christ into the world.

This notion of the church as body counters the modern tendency to close our lives off from one another. It calls us to powerful expressions of community. Ten recent college graduates in Camden, New Jersey, have been inspired by this ideal to set up Camden House, a home where they share much more than just rent. Each day they gather for worship and prayer. They split up the chores and take turns preparing meals. Even though these people work at different places and earn different salaries, they place all their earnings in a common collection. From this collection they pay their bills and contribute a weekly tithe to assist the residents of their depressed neighborhood. On the weekends, house members share projects that model Christian community. One of the most creative ministries of Camden House is called Eve's Gardens. These are vegetable gardens grown on rooftops and abandoned lots. The produce grown there is shared with those in need, and the plots themselves provide visual reminders of God's creation—tiny green islands in a sea of concrete.

> *"Your pain is my pain. My wealth is your wealth. Your salvation is my salvation."*
>
> *African Proverb*

While most Christians may not open their lives to one another in such dramatic ways, many are discovering anew the power of a shared life. In one of Mark's congregations, the youth group held a "Body of Christ Auction." With the tag line "We All Have a Hand in the Body of Christ," youth auctioned themselves off as babysitters, car washers, and lawn crews. A youth who enjoyed performing magic tricks offered to provide a show for small children. Another youth, who studied art, offered to draw a family portrait. The day of the auction was great fun. Small children got into bidding wars with their parents. Auctioneers entertained everyone with jokes and skits. Volunteers received pies in the face from the highest bidders. When the day was over, the youth raised enough money to fund a summer mission trip. On that trip they "reinvested" the money they collected by trimming hedges, building wheelchair ramps, and painting the houses of those in need. The same event that brought Mark's congregation closer together provided an opportunity for the youth to share Christ's love in tangible ways.

"Christ has no body now but yours, no hands but yours, no feet but yours. Yours are the eyes through which the compassion of Christ is to look out on a hurting world. Yours are the feet with which he is to go about doing good. Yours are the hands with which he is to bless now."

Teresa of Avila

LEARNING TO RECEIVE

In his book *The Gift,* cultural anthropologist Marcel Mauss describes how in pre-modern societies one person gave gifts on behalf of the tribe or village to someone who received them on behalf of another tribe or village. The Big Man of one tribe might, for example, give a basket of cowry shells to the Big Man in another tribe. In such societies the gift exchange performed a very important function. The sharing provided a way for the two communities to honor each other. For the system to work, it carried with it not only an obligation to give but also to receive.

Receiving gifts gratefully and joyfully is one of the most important things we can do to build Christian community. Yet, for many of us it is much harder to receive a gift than to give one. What is the first thing that many of us say when someone gives us an unexpected gift? "You shouldn't have!" Why do we say that? Perhaps it is because some small part of us wishes that the giver had not done it. Simply by receiving, we feel obligated, even indebted; and that makes many of us uncomfortable.

In one of Wendell Berry's stories, a farmhand named Elton receives the surprising gift of a farm when Jack Beecham, his boss and landowner, passes away. At first, Elton is thrilled with this unexpected inheritance; but then it starts to make him feel uneasy. Berry describes Elton's growing ambivalence: "Like any young man who has won his heart's desire, Elton wishes he had won it by himself, wishes to possess it on his own terms, its first and only lover."

One day, a wise country lawyer named Wheeler comes to see Elton on his new farm. Elton explains his dilemma to the lawyer: "I want to make it on my own, I don't want a soul to thank." Wheeler thinks, "Too late," but he does not say it. Instead he grins. "Well," he says, ... I don't think your old friend has left you in shape to live thankless." Elton says, "What do you mean?" "I mean you're a man indebted to a dead man. So am I. So was he. That's the story of it. Back of you is Jack Beecham. Back of him was Ben Feltner. Back of him was, I think, his own daddy. And back of him somebody else, and on back that way, who knows how far? ... It's no use to want to make it on your own, because you can't. ... You're in a different line of succession."[5]

Part of following Jesus Christ is coming to the realization that there is no such thing as a self-made woman or man. Like Elton, we learn that our "line of succession" is much longer than we had ever realized. Part of the purpose of this study is to help us acknowledge our indebtedness to the first generation of believers who handed the faith down to us through a long succession of faithful followers. Behind all of them stands the God of Jesus Christ, the One who started all of it with the gift of grace. The only way to respond to such indebtedness is to follow Wheeler's advice. We can give up trying to live a thankless life and begin to see that everything we do, everything we have to share, is an expression of gratitude and joy. The body of Christ is not complete and true sharing does not begin until this final lesson is learned.

STONE SOUP

We are invited to gather around the fire and experience the warmth of a life opened to God and others. This spirit of openness, of learning to give and to receive, is expressed in the old mountain fable "Stone Soup":

Once upon a time, a great famine swept all across the hills. The people became so scared that they hoarded their possessions. They hid their food from persons who used to be their dearest friends. One day a man wandered into the village. He asked if he could stay the night. "Oh no! Don't stay here," the villagers replied. "There is not a bite to eat in the whole province. You better keep moving on."

"That's alright," the stranger replied. "I have everything I need. In fact, I was thinking of making some stone soup to share with all of you." He pulled an iron cauldron from his wagon, filled it with water, and built a fire under it. Then, with great ceremony, he drew an ordinary-looking stone from a burlap bag and dropped it into the water.

By now, hearing the rumor of food, most of the villagers came out to watch. "Ah," the stranger said loudly to himself, "I do like a tasty stone soup. Of course, stone soup with cabbage—that's hard to beat."

Soon a villager approached hesitantly, holding a cabbage he'd retrieved from its hiding place, and added it to the pot. "Wonderful!" cried the stranger. "You know, I once had stone soup with cabbage and a bit of salt beef as well, and it was fit for a king." The village butcher managed to find some salt beef … and so it went, through potatoes, onions, carrots, mushrooms, and so on, until everyone had shared and everyone had received the gift of the entire community. As the stranger left town, the villagers begged him to leave the magic stone behind because they were very hungry. He explained that the stone was not necessary. All the magic they needed was in their openness to give and to receive.[6]

---

1. From *Two Weeks' Notice*, written and directed by Lawrence (Castlerock Entertainment, 2002).

2. From *The Geography of Nowhere,* by James Kuntsler. Quoted in *Affluenza: The All-Consuming Epidemic,* by John de Graaf, David Wann, and Thomas H. Naylor (Berrett-Koehler Publishers, 2001); pages 60–61.

3. From *God's Beloved: A Spiritual Biography of Henri Nouwen,* by Michael O'Laughlin (Orbis, 2004); page 140.

4. From *The Road to Daybreak: A Spiritual Journey,* by Henri J. M. Nouwen (Doubleday, 1988); page 7.

5. From "It Wasn't Me," in *That Distant Land: The Collected Stories,* by Wendell Berry (Shoemaker and Hoard, 2004); pages 282–84.

6. Traditional Tale.

Seven: How Can We Remember Who We Are?

Worship

"Day by day, the followers of Jesus Christ spent much time together in the temple in Jerusalem."

(Acts 2:46a, authors' translation)

WORSHIPING ALONE

A number of years ago, Andy traveled to Egypt to climb to the top of Mount Sinai, where tradition tells us Moses received the Ten Commandments. Andy experienced worshiping God alone:

> Everyone else with whom I had traveled to the Middle East had gone home. I had scheduled a few extra days at the end of my trip to see Mount Sinai. Ever since I saw Charlton Heston in *The Ten Commandments,* I wanted to climb that mountain and see the sun rise over the Sinai. At the Israeli-Egyptian border, I joined a two-jeep caravan tour to the site. I was the only American and the only Christian in our group. We arrived at several small concrete shelters at the base of the mountain late in the afternoon. After a hot meal, everyone eventually went to sleep under blankets on uncomfortable cots.
>
> At 3:00 AM our guides woke us up, gave us some hot tea and biscuits, and began to lead us up the steep mountain. To travel light, I left my backpack at the bottom of the mountain. The air was frigid and thin, and the guides kept urging us not to stop. Just before 6:00 AM, we made it to the top just in time. Watching the sun rise over the rugged mountains of the Sinai Peninsula took my breath away; it felt

> as if I were seeing God. I had achieved my dream. Yet, I also experienced a profound sense of regret. I was by myself, in a strange land, not knowing the local language, and with no friends or family with whom to share this experience. I had even left my Bible in my backpack, so I was unable to reread the story of Moses. I was experiencing God alone without any sense of reference. I never wish to feel that loss of community and sense of isolation again.

At times all of us share some spiritual amnesia, feeling alone, having forgotten who we are and whose we are. This spiritual amnesia results when we view our traditions as unnecessary restraints. Having lost our roots, we value self-interest and self-concern more than remembering who and what has formed us into the persons we are. For example, in our relationship with God many of us believe that we can best worship God individually while standing on top of a mountain, or walking on the beach, or closeted in our homes. Closing ourselves off on a private retreat may seem to give us more access to God than being surrounded by other people and hearing ancient stories, or saying traditional words, or singing old hymns in worship. Yet, while these private moments do have their place in our spiritual lives, they allow us to forget the very God we worship.

HOMECOMING

Compare Andy's private worship experience on Mount Sinai with another worship experience. In many congregations the highlight of the year is Homecoming. At Jonas Ridge, North Carolina, Baptist and United Methodist families and friends gather from far and near on the second Sunday of July each year. People greet each other with hugs and kisses. Families visit inside the two old, white sanctuaries that stand side by side; and they walk through the old graveyard. Standing amidst the tombstones, older members tell the children stories about past people and events. Food is brought out of car trunks and displayed on old folding tables that groan under the weight. At the climax of the day, the community gathers in the sanctuaries to hear the Bible read and preached and to sing "Bless Be the Tie That Binds."

> *"The physical presence of other Christians is a source of incomparable joy and strength to the believer."*
>
> *Dietrich Bonhoeffer*

Gathering with other people for celebration and remembrance is an essential part of being human. No one wants to celebrate a birthday alone. A family or school reunion gets better and better with more and more people. While a wedding anniversary may be celebrated by a couple alone, when families come together for the fiftieth anniversary of a beloved couple, generations of friends and family find the event electric. National anniversaries—whether to remember a tragedy such as 9/11 or a landmark event such as the Fourth of July—are best celebrated, not at home alone, but on the public square, where speakers evoke memories and the physical presence of others forms community. In the church, worship lights the fire that gathers us together with each other and with God.

On Palm Sunday 1994, the small congregation of Goshen United Methodist Church in Piedmont, Alabama, gathered in their sanctuary to hear the children sing an Easter musical. A tornado suddenly struck the building. The brick walls of the building collapsed. Twenty people—children, women, and men—died, including Hannah Clem, the young daughter of pastor Kelly Clem. In the midst of her intense grief, interviewers asked Pastor Clem, "Why?" She responded, "I don't know why. There are no easy answers." Throughout the week, one funeral followed another. Would the community of faith survive this tragic disaster?

The answer arrived on the following Sunday. On Easter, just one week after the tornado, the Goshen congregation gathered again in the parking lot of the destroyed sanctuary. As the sun rose and broke through the darkness, members of the congregation came together as a family; and Pastor Clem read the story of Jesus' resurrection from the dead. With the stark reality of death before them, the congregation then sang together, "Because he lives, I can face tomorrow." Worship has the power to evoke redemptive memories. Through their worship, the healing had begun.

"We will not forget."
Kelly Clem

AN ANTIDOTE TO AMNESIA

Worship serves as an antidote to our spiritual amnesia. Enabling a community to gather and connect with one another, worship also helps us remember and center our lives on the stories of God. Ultimately, worship orients our lives to serve the world and sends us forth as disciples of Jesus Christ.

What is worship? Many definitions exist. For example, in one definition the word *worship* means "giving worth to someone in authority." In Christian community, worship means giving honor and glory to God. Worship may also be understood as a "means of grace" through which God bestows upon people all the gifts of the Holy Spirit they need in their journey with God. Worship provides a way of communicating God's love and opens for us the possibility of transformation.

A newspaper columnist described worship in this way:

> Faith is not me and God alone. Baptism puts me in a community of believers. Though they can be irritating, exasperating and occasionally cruel, they continually teach me that to love others means loving—and forgiving—those who can be unlovable. Though sermons don't always inspire, they do connect me to a worldview that rises above the clamor I'm drowning in day after day. On a good Sunday, a sermon readjusts my perspective on life and renews hope. Hymns allow me to give expression to buried emotions. Their tunes direct my praise to the One who is the Author of all that is. Without

> such outward expressions, I can easily become obsessed with self. Prayers remind me that life isn't only about me. A community of faith is made up of individuals with joys, pains and desires that are unknown to others unless expressed. Petitions to God become opportunities for service and celebration. I stay connected to church because it connects me with the One who loves me, and compels me to do the same for others. I know churches aren't perfect. Never will be.... Sometimes it takes the eyes and ears of faith to recognize the presence of God in a church.[1]

THE FIRST CHRISTIANS AT WORSHIP

After the Day of Pentecost, the first Christians also found it necessary to remember God. The first fever of the Holy Spirit began to run down. The everydayness of life dampened their passion. Besieged by aggressive authorities, they were tempted to remain isolated from one another and simply thank God in private moments for the experience of Pentecost. Yet, they did not worship God alone in the back alleys of Jerusalem but publicly and boldly.

> "And let us consider how we may spur one another on toward love and good deeds, not giving up meeting together, as some are in the habit of doing, but encouraging one another."
>
> (Hebrews 10:24-25a)

How did those first Christians worship? They gathered every day at the rising of the sun and the lighting of the evening lamps to sing psalms and spiritual hymns and to offer prayers. To show that they were different from their Jewish neighbors, the early followers said the Lord's Prayer and celebrated the resurrection of Jesus Christ on the first day of the week, which we now call Sunday. They baptized one another in the name of the Father, the Son, and the Holy Spirit and ate together in a holy meal with bread and a cup of wine. As they worshiped in all these ways, the people of Pentecost kept the fire of faith flaming.

REMEMBERING GOD

Each of those early and continuing ways of worship describes God's mighty acts from Creation to the final days and invites us into a new reality. As we hear the biblical narratives describing the beginning of the universe to the last moments of Creation, we find that worship reframes our lives so that we do not see ourselves in the story of economy and commerce, needs and worries, traffic jams, and what we are having for supper. Worship reminds us of the all-encompassing story of a loving God who longs for us to be in relationship with that same living God and everyone who shares our faith.

How does worship connect us with God? As we sing songs, profess our faith, participate in the sacraments, offer our gifts, and involve ourselves in a host of other activities, we participate anew in the narratives and the doctrines of our faith. While worship is not primarily an intellectual venture, worshipers grow in their knowledge of God and the ways in which this knowledge intersects and transforms life.

In worship we become a part of God's story, especially when we are attentive to God's Word. Sometimes we forget the power of the divine narrative. In one of Andy's congregations, a bright young man joined the church. His parents had not reared him as a Christian. Having received graduate degrees in counseling, he had become a talented caregiver. After attending the church for several years, he came forward to be baptized and join the community. He read voluminously and always had interesting questions to ask. Andy recalls:

> One day my new friend called and asked a fascinating question. He said that he had noticed that every Sunday I read a passage from the Bible and then spoke about the meaning of that passage. He had just read a great article in *The New York Times Book Review* and wondered if I would like to read an excerpt from an article and use that passage as the basis of my next sermon. Suggesting that maybe I

should branch out, he said, "Andy, you don't need to read only one book in worship." At that moment, I realized that he did not know what the Bible was and why it stood at the center of our worship life. And I suspected that he was not alone.

Throughout the ages, people have reconnected with God when they gathered around the Word of God. In the Old Testament, when the Temple in Jerusalem fell into disrepair, King Josiah began to restore the place of worship. In the midst of the renovations, the workers discovered a lost scroll, a parchment of animal skin rolled together that contained the first five books of the Bible. "Then the king called together all the elders of Judah and Jerusalem. He went up to the temple of the LORD with the people of Judah . . . all the people from the least to the greatest. He read in their hearing all the words of the Book of the Covenant" (2 Chronicles 34:29-30). A spiritual revival ensued.

At the beginning of his ministry, Jesus returned to his hometown of Nazareth and went into the synagogue, the place of worship. Then Jesus "stood up to read, and the scroll of the prophet Isaiah was handed to him. Unrolling it, he found the place" (Luke 4:16-17) and read aloud the Word of God. Immediately, Jesus established his place in God's history.

"Worship, then, is an avenue which leads the creature out from his inveterate self-occupation to a knowledge of God, and ultimately to that union with God which is the beatitude of the soul."

Evelyn Underhill

THE WORD OF GOD

What is this "Word of God"? The Word of God has a variety of meanings. It defines first and foremost Jesus Christ, as expressed in the first chapter of John, in which Jesus Christ himself is revealed as the very person of God. Beyond the person of Jesus Christ, the Word of God also refers to the whole of the Christian Scriptures, traditionally called the Old and New Testaments. [Discussed in *Along the Way,* Chapter 5, by Andy Langford and Mark Ralls (Abingdon Press, 2003).] When a congregation reads the Bible in worship, the Word of God becomes present and real. Beyond these first two meanings, the Word of God also applies to the spoken interpretation of the Bible, often called the sermon, which links the Scripture with contemporary human life.

How are we attentive to the Word of God in our worship? One major way of reading the Bible in worship involves the use of a lectionary, a table of readings from the Bible that over a period of time covers much of the Bible in a systematic way. Other methods of being attentive to Scripture include working through one book of the Bible, focusing on one set of themes, or responding to personal and communal events by finding appropriate passages from the Bible.

Another way of being attentive to the Word is observing the Christian year. As a congregation follows the Christian year from Advent to Pentecost, it hears the whole of Jesus' story: anticipation of the Messiah (Advent), his birth (Christmas), presentation to the nations (Epiphany), baptism, transfiguration (Transfiguration), passion (Lent), death (Holy Week), resurrection (Easter), ascension, and the coming of the Holy Spirit upon the community of faith (Pentecost). As the Christian year unfolds, we journey with Jesus Christ to his final triumph.

When we engage with God's Word in Scripture, we move out of our isolation and into God's story.

GOOD WORSHIP?

As with baptism and Holy Communion, sometimes we in the church let our differences over worship divide us. What should the pastor wear? What dress code should the congregation observe? Which translation of the Bible must we read? What music will we play? Which hymns or songs will we sing? What is the appropriate role for women? Should children be present or have their own separate space? Which creed should we profess? Should we sit in straight rows in hard pews or in soft chairs in the round? Sometimes arguments about worship can split a congregation.

Worship exists in a wide variety of styles. Christians around the world worship in many liturgical traditions. Every tradition and style of worship has strengths and weaknesses and serves a particular group of people. There are as many kinds of appropriate worship as there are congregations of faithful followers of Jesus Christ. Scripture does not define in precise terms how we should worship. Much of what many people believe is essential to worship consists primarily of traditions that have developed over the millennia. For example, the Bible encourages us to sing; but it does not express a preference for a hymn accompanied by an organ, or unaccompanied by any instrument, or backed up by drums, keyboards, and guitars. What is fundamental is that we must worship.

"If you scorn the fellowship of the brethren, you reject the call of Jesus Christ."

Dietrich Bonhoeffer

WAYS THAT WORSHIP OVERCOMES OUR AMNESIA

When we remember God as those first Christians did and gather around the Word of God in whatever style we observe, worship serves us in several ways: as a compass, as a soundtrack, and as a rehearsal stage for life. Some people describe worship as "getting a boost" or "filling up on God" for the coming week. Other people worship because they enjoy the music or the setting or the fellowship. Some folks worship to be with other people. Others simply come out of habit. In the movie *Sister Act,* Whoopi Goldberg's character states that the purpose of worship is to "get some butts in the seats." [2] All these explanations have some weight, but ultimately they are not enough.

We often underestimate the power of worship. As Annie Dillard, a modern-day Christian mystic, reminds us, "I do not find Christians, outside the catacombs [caves in Rome where early Christians worshiped and were buried], sufficiently sensible, aware of conditions. Does anyone have the foggiest idea what sort of power we so blindly invoke? Or, as I suspect, does no one believe a word of it? The churches are children, playing on the floor with their chemistry sets, mixing up a batch of TNT to kill a Sunday morning."[3]

What is the explosive power of worship? Worship sometimes functions like a compass, keeping us oriented toward God. Navigators at sea or on land do not check their compass because it is entertaining, or a really nice compass, or "the same kind of compass my great, great grandfather owned." Navigators check compasses to orient themselves toward their intended destination. Every ritual and litany, every song and drama, every sermon and sacrament, orients God's people toward God and helps to build communal life around that shared orientation.

In their book *Resident Aliens,* Stanley Hauerwas and Will Willimon suggest:

> The church at worship continues to be the acid test.... In our worship, we retell and are held accountable to God's story, the adventure story about what God is doing with us in Christ. All ministry can be evaluated by essentially liturgical criteria: How well does the act of ministry enable people to be with God? In worship, in preaching, in serving the Lord's Supper, in baptizing, the pastor receives the model

> whereby all other pastoral acts are to be judged, the pattern into which all other ministerial duties are to be fit, namely, orienting God's people to God.[4]

Worship also functions as a soundtrack that hums gently in the background of our daily lives. When we shop or go to restaurants or attend sporting events, we often hear in the background of that activity some music that intensifies the experience. The music in a restaurant may soothe us, while the songs at a basketball game bring us to our feet. When we worship, we develop a way of seeing the world that affects everything we do. For example, "A Statement of Faith From the United Church of Canada" names the core of the biblical witness:

> We are not alone, we live in God's world.
> We believe in God:
> who has created and is creating
> who has come in Jesus, the Word made flesh,
>   to reconcile and make new,
>   who works in us and others by the Spirit.
> We trust in God.
> We are called to be the church:
> to celebrate God's presence,
> to love and serve others,
> to seek justice and resist evil,
> to proclaim Jesus crucified and risen,
> our judge and our hope.
> In life in death, in life beyond death,
> God is with us.
> We are not alone.
> Thanks be to God. Amen.[5]

When we say words such as these over and over again in our worship, they become a soundtrack, a background against which we see the world.

"The words with which we praise God shape the world in which we shall live."

Walter Brueggemann

Finally, worship invites us to a rehearsal before the big performance. What we hear, say, do, and experience within a community of believers becomes the way we live throughout our lives. We are not just entertainers on the stage for an hour a week; we are actors in the divine drama that happens 24/7/365. In this drama, God participates on the stage with us and sits in the audience as we play our roles. Priests, preachers, musicians, and other worship leaders prompt the people of God at worship, aiding the gathered body of Christ in performing the act of worship for the Holy One, becoming knit together with other members of the body of Christ. For example, if we say in worship, "I forgive you," forgiveness may become a way of life for us during the week. In this way, worship leads to the continual resurrection and life of Christ in the world.

"Unless the few of us who know the truth ... stand united, there is no hope for any of us."

Headmaster Albus Dumbledore

Think about how congregational singing binds us together in the holy drama of worship. The act of singing Christian songs together is a practice unparalleled in secular society, with the possible exception of singing a national anthem (which today has become more of a spectator sport than a participatory activity). Yet, when Christians join their voices to sing "Holy, Holy, Holy" or "Amazing Grace, How Sweet the Sound" or "Our God Is a Mighty God," we are knit together as a community.

"In worship we receive the self-giving love of God, and the test of our thankfulness is whether we reproduce that pattern

of self-giving in our daily relationships with other people. Of course, the test already begins with our attitudes and behaviors as brothers and sisters in the liturgical assembly."

Geoffrey Wainwright

DOES WORSHIP WORK?

"Worship is one of the most profound experiences of life for humankind. For Christians, gathering around the Lord's Table, the baptismal font, and the scriptures are essential elements of an authentic life."

Reuben Job

Rob tells the story of a man who attended his congregation:

A member of our congregation was facing surgery. During our worship service on the day before his surgery, I invited our children to gather in the front of our worship area. I asked this man to come and sit with us. He and I sat on the floor in the midst of the children. I told the children the story of this man coming to be a part of our community and what God was doing in his life. I shared with them that he was going to have a very serious surgery the next day and we needed to pray for him. The children and I placed our hands on him as we prayed for his healing. As I prayed a simple prayer, the children repeated my prayer line by line. When we finished praying, I don't think there was a dry eye in the sanctuary. Worship engages us in the activities that proclaim what we believe; and as we participate, we are formed.

"Going to church is like approaching an open volcano, where the world is molten and hearts are sifted. The altar is like a rail that splatters sparks, the sanctuary like the chamber next to an atomic oven; there are invisible rays, and you leave your watch outside."

Amos Wilder

Andy remembers:

Several years ago I attended worship at Glide Memorial United Methodist Church in San Francisco. The exterior of the church looked much like its neighborhood, an area called the Tenderloin District. Within this area of San Francisco every kind of human flesh was for sale. When I entered the building, men and women in rough blue jeans greeted us. Plywood covered the stained-glass windows. Banners made with flannel and glue, filled with words such as *Hope* and *Respect,* hung on the walls. Multicolored strobe lights beamed down from the balcony.

The most remarkable aspect, however, was the congregation. Some older persons wore traditional Sunday clothes. But well-dressed people were the exception. Most of the people in the congregation came in separately and sat alone; several appeared to be prostitutes. Other men and women had a dazed, lost look on their faces, while other folk simply looked exhausted. Throughout the service, the pastor encouraged the people and invited them to pray for their needs. Voices raised in prayer asked for a cure for AIDS, for recovery from addiction, and for food. The preacher declared, "God does not make trash. God does not own a trash can." At the close of worship, the congregation moved down the hall to the soup kitchen run by that congregation. Glide Memorial's worship broke almost every rule of traditional worship, yet I could feel the presence of the Holy Spirit. We belonged to each other. We belonged to God.

PREPARING FOR WORSHIP

In Andy's congregation, a small group of women gather each week in the sanctuary. For several years, they have met on Wednesday mornings to prepare that place for worship. They do not gather to pick up leftover bulletins, or to sharpen the pencils in the pews, or to rearrange the chairs. They gather to pray. As they individually enter, each woman begins by kneeling before the Communion Table and praying for the whole congregation. Then each woman slowly walks to each part of the worship space and prays—to the pulpit to pray for the preacher, to the organ to pray for the musician, to the choir loft to pray for the singers, to the lectern to pray for the other worship leaders, to each pew to pray for the people who will sit there on Sunday, to the offering plates to pray that the money collected will be used for the kingdom of God, to each of the doors to pray for everyone who enters for the first time. Surrounded and infusing the sanctuary with prayer, they create an environment that transforms Sunday worship.

How should we prepare for worship? Pray for the service and for the worship leaders. Read the Bible and listen to God's Word. Think of the people who will sit beside us. Get our offering ready for God. With such preparation, Sunday worship may be transformed.

THE POWER OF WORSHIP

Can worship together really make a difference? Can music, corporate prayers, affirmations of faith, and hearing the Word of God truly help us remember who we are? A newspaper columnist once gave this answer:

> What drew me back to the church after years of wandering? I needed to be part of a caring community. . . . Few organizations can provide the intimate connections I find in church. With other members of our congregation, I experience the full measure of life. Babies are born and welcomed into our church family. Strangers join us and become friends. Elders die and are laid to rest in the company of the congregation. We differ in many ways, but we share a belief about what's important in life and what we are to each other.[6]

As Don Saliers, a beloved professor, once wrote, "It's like you dream . . . a vision . . . that people gather for prayer, worshiping, offering praise, thanksgiving, the music, the responding, singing. At some point they say 'we could stay here forever.' That's the kingdom."[7]

---

1. From "Why I Go to Church," by Tom Schaefer, in *The Charlotte Observer,* June 13, 2005; page 11A.

2. From *Sister Act*, screenplay by Joseph Howard (1992).

3. From *Holy the Firm,* by Annie Dillard (Harper & Row, 1984); page 4.

4. From *Resident Aliens,* by Stanley Hauerwas and Will Willimon (Abingdon Press, 1989); pages 138–39.

5. From *The United Methodist Hymnal* (Copyright © 1989 by The United Methodist Publishing House); 883.

6. From "Some Thoughts About Life, Death, and Thereafter," by Ed Williams, in *The Charlotte Observer,* January 25, 2004; page D-3.

7. From *Worship as Theology,* by Don Saliers (Abingdon Press, 1994); page 145.

Eight: How Can We Open Our Lives to Each Other?

Hospitality

"The invitation that we as Christians extend to one another is not simply an invitation into our homes . . . ; what we ask of other people is that they enter into our lives."

Lauren Winner

"They shared meals together from home to home."

(Acts 2:46b, authors' paraphrase)

"And let us consider how we may spur one another on toward love and good deeds, not giving up meeting together, as some are in the habit of doing, but encouraging one another."

(Hebrews 10:24-25a)

STRANGERS

In Frederick Buechner's novel *Love Feast,* a traveling evangelist named Leo Bebb hosts a Thanksgiving party for those who have nowhere else to celebrate the holiday. Sitting around the table are college students and retirees, nuns and secretaries, hookers and the homeless. When this odd assortment of guests have finished their meal, Leo stands at the head of the table and wonders aloud why we find it so difficult to open our lives to one another: "There's strangers everywhere you can think of. There's strangers was born out of the same womb. There's strangers was raised together in the same town and worked side by side all their life through. There's strangers got married and been climbing in and out of the same four poster together for thirty-five or forty years, and they're strangers still."[1]

Leo Bebb may have put his finger on the problem of our age. We no longer seem to have the time or energy to connect with each other. Earlier generations, for instance, often visited in each other's homes. Friends dropped by to share the events of the day. Neighbors sat around the kitchen table drinking coffee. Families entertained one another in the parlor.

Things are different today. If you doubt this, tune into Nickelodeon and watch *I Love Lucy* sometime. Notice how often Lucy and Ricky, Fred and Ethyl, are in each other's apartments. Check out how they are intimately involved in each other's lives. How does this compare with your relationships? Many of us would struggle even to name the neighbor who lives down the hall. Most of us have never been inside the home of the family across the street. It seems that we are losing our ability to let others into our homes and into our lives. We feel more like strangers than ever before.

The ancient Hebrews used the same word for *stranger* and *border*. This was no coincidence. Strangers are persons who could have been friends if only we had dared to invite them across the imaginary boundary between us. We waste so much time maintaining boundaries because of mistaken assumptions and insecurities.

We assume that one day we will have more time to cultivate relationships than we do now. Life will always be demanding and busy, however; just ask a recent retiree if she has a lot of extra time on her hands! If we cannot find the time and energy to begin reaching out to others now, chances are we never will. We assume that our homes are too messy to invite others in and that our lives are too disorderly to open up to others. Yet, if we are holding out for a Good Housekeeping Seal of Approval or some sign from above that we finally have it all together, we will miss out on the best part of friendship: the knowledge that we are loved and accepted for who we are! Finally, we assume that if other persons do not take the initiative, they are not interested in our friendship. We forget that others struggle with the same challenges, distractions, and insecurities that we do. In most cases they are just like us. They are waiting to be invited.

> *"In our world full of strangers, estranged . . . from their neighbors, friends and family, from their deepest self and their God, we witness a painful search for a hospitable place . . . where community can be found."*
>
> *Henri Nouwen*

We struggle to see through our own assumptions and insecurities, and because of this we never really connect. Carrie Newcomer expresses it well in her song "Nomads." She sings, "We're like waves out on the water / we touch and then move away." [2]

Life does not have to be this way. As followers of Christ, we are committed to border crossings. Christ calls us to invite those who are strangers into our homes and into our lives. As we take this risk, we discover a new reality that Leo Bebb describes as he continues his after-dinner speech: "The Kingdom of Heaven is a love feast where nobody's a stranger. Like right here. . . . Here in this place there's no strangers. . . . It's like every one of us has lost his way so bad we don't even know which way is home any more only we're ashamed to ask. You know what would happen if we would own up we're lost and ask? Why, what would happen is we'd find home is each other. We'd find home is Jesus loves us lost found or any whichway."[3]

CHRISTIAN HOSPITALITY

> *"That is our vocation; to convert . . . the enemy into a guest and to create the free and fearless space where brotherhood and sisterhood can be formed and fully experienced."*
>
> *Henri Nouwen*

The first generation of Christians discovered through the practice of hospitality that "home is each other." When we think of hospitality, we may imagine the so-called hospitality industry: hotels and resorts, spas and cruise ships. We think of smiling attendants catering to our needs and helping us to feel at home even when we are not. This example shares something of what the early Christians meant by hospitality. It shares a readiness to serve and to treat others with attentive care and respect. Yet, there is one big difference. Our contemporary version of hospitality comes with strings attached. Hospitality is offered only to those who can pay for it. It is an exchange. Although the respect and care we receive may be genuine, hospitality is extended only to those with a reservation and a credit card.

Early Christian hospitality, on the other hand, came with no strings attached. The first Christians modeled their practice after the example of Jesus Christ. Jesus chafed against the limits of social propriety by welcoming prostitutes and adulterers, crooks and outcasts, into friendship. In his teachings, Jesus urged hosts to invite more than family and friends to the dinner table. He said that Christians should give banquets to the poor and the sick, to people who have nothing to offer the host in return. Jesus even went so far as to promise that when we welcome a stranger or feed a hungry person, we are befriending him (Matthew 25:31-40).

When the first generation of Christians practiced hospitality, they sought to model themselves after the way that Jesus welcomed strangers as guests and transformed them into friends. This understanding of hospitality set early Christians apart from their surrounding culture. Non-Christians of their day also prized hospitality; but, as with much contemporary hosting, it always had strings attached. Hospitality was directed toward family, friends, and influential social contacts—those who could easily reciprocate the host's goodwill. Christian hospitality was quite different. Not only were all welcome, it was those least likely to reciprocate (widows, orphans, and foreigners) who were its primary recipients. Christian hospitality cut against the grain of social propriety. In a world where most of us live as strangers, the first generation of Christians modeled a new way of life that cultivated friendships with all.

THE HOUSEHOLD OF GOD

"Home is the place where, when you have to go there,
They have to take you in."

Robert Frost

Households were the most important location for early Christian hospitality. This development occurred naturally. The family home, after all, was the center of both Jewish and Greek life. When individuals from these traditions became Christians, they carried with them the assumption that the household would be the hub of religious, social, and political life. Yet, they added to this assumption a new theological understanding. Paul, for instance, considered Christians to be a new family of believers whose life together is characterized by an overflowing of mutual affection (1 Thessalonians 3:12). The author of First Peter put it even more explicitly. The church, he said, is nothing less than "God's household" (1 Peter 4:17). The church was a new household, made up of the family of God. Believers were not only invited into intimate fellowship with one another; they were expected to become like family to one another.

Since the family life of this household is modeled after Jesus, it is characterized by openness. The basis of Christian community is not the ties of blood or kinship. Rather, it is a divine call to create a new and open family. Through Christ, God has made us into one family. Jesus Christ is the source of our life together. This means that we not only see each other as brothers and sisters in Christ; we also recognize that potential in everyone who crosses our path. The first

Christians expressed this commitment in a variety of ways. For instance, in each city where Christians lived, one or more families made their homes available for the assembly of the community (Acts 12:12; Romans 16:3-5; Colossians 4:15). Christians worshiped together there, shared meals, and held informal conversations. These homes were also vital centers of support for missionaries and other Christians who may have been traveling through the city. The structure of this new, open household transcended the notions of family ties from Greek and Jewish culture and created a place where Christian hospitality could be practiced in concrete ways.

> *"Home is not a sanctuary from the world, but a place within the world where we go to understand our responsibility to it."*
> *Craig Barnes*

Not too many years ago, archeologists excavated an ancient Christian church in the biblical town of Capernaum. Jesus stayed in this town on the north shore of the Sea of Galilee in the home of his disciple Peter, where he healed Peter's mother-in-law. Digging through several layers of plaster, researchers discovered Christian symbols scrawled on the walls, including the names Jesus and Peter. They began to wonder if underneath this church, dating back to the fourth century, was the actual home of Peter. When archeologists finally reached the original foundation, they discovered broken shards of pottery and fishhooks on the floor and a small fire pit. At the center of the church was a home with a hearth. It was fitting. Since the days of the earliest Christians, the home has been a place of belonging and hospitality, a place of mutual affection and open acceptance, a place to gather around the fire.

CONTEMPORARY CHRISTIAN HOSPITALITY

All around us there are examples of communities seeking to live out the profound implications of our Christian identity as the household of God. Dorothy Day was the founder of a Catholic community in the 1930s. Her commitment to hospitality has remained a powerful influence for many followers of Jesus Christ. When her Catholic Worker houses began providing shelter to homeless persons, Day was often criticized. Some said that she was indiscriminate in selecting those helped, choosing to assist drunkards and hobos rather than more "deserving" folks. "How long," she was pointedly asked, "are you going to let these people stay in your homes?" "We let them stay forever," Dorothy Day replied tersely. "They live with us, they die with us, and we give them a Christian burial. We pray for them after they are dead. Once they are taken in, they become members of the family. . . . They are our brothers and sisters in Christ."[4]

Many communities today consider themselves to be the spiritual heirs of Dorothy Day. Among them is Jubilee Partners, a Christian residential community in the mountains of north Georgia. During the past twenty years, Jubilee Partners has welcomed over two thousand refugees driven from their homes by war. People have come there from Thailand, Nicaragua, South Africa, Bosnia, and Iraq. Jubilee residents pool their resources to provide these persons with housing, food; English lessons; and, most importantly, a community of love and acceptance. Their goal is to scatter seeds of peace by making space for residents and refugees to share life together.

While they may be carrying out hospitality in less dramatic ways, many Christians are changing lives by opening themselves to others. Hospitality is as much an attitude as an activity. It is an expression of *ubuntu,* an openness to the other that quietly counteracts our contemporary culture of strangers. Andy remembers his Grandmother Langford as a gentle yet persistent catalyst for hospitality:

> Grandmother lived in the same house for forty years. Each afternoon she would sit on her front porch, rock, read the afternoon paper, and visit with neighbors walking down the sidewalk just a few feet from her porch. Grandmother knew by name every one of her neighbors and shared with everyone news about everyone else. When she

moved from her home into a modern apartment complex (the old home just needed too much work), she again put a rocking chair on the front porch, which in this case was just five feet of concrete next to a parking lot, and greeted all her new neighbors when they arrived home after work. Within weeks, Grandmother had introduced everyone in her new residence to everyone else; and a sterile apartment building had become a community.

A SOCIETY OF FRIENDS

"In this world two things are essential: a healthy life and friendship. God created humans so that they might exist and live: this is life. But if they are not to remain solitary, there must be friendship."

Augustine

What all of these Christian hosts have in common—from Dorothy Day to Andy's grandmother—is that they risked opening their lives to others. As they did this, the Holy Spirit created a new reality, a community of transformation where strangers could become guests and guests could eventually become friends. Friendship is always the goal of Christian hospitality.

A friend is something more than a temporary guest. Friends have a special place in our lives. We share a bond with them that is deep and lasting. Once again our model is found in an invitation from Jesus Christ. Shortly before he was arrested and then crucified, Jesus gathered his disciples together and told them this: "You are my friends if you do what I command. I no longer call you servants, because servants do not know their master's business. Instead, I have called you friends, for everything that I have learned from my Father I have made known to you.... This is my command: Love each other" (John 15:14-17). As followers of Jesus, we are invited to be his friend.

What does it mean to be a friend of Jesus? It means that God includes us in an intimate, mutually supportive community with

Jesus Christ at its center. We are part of a new reality and have a new identity. We are now Jesus' friends, and this truth about us changes all our relationships. In other words, this friendship is never "just me and Jesus." It is always directed outward, calling us to open ourselves to Jesus' most important command: "Love each other."

The Greek philosopher Aristotle said that friendship occurs when two people perceive something good in each other that leads them to love each other. A Christ-centered friendship does not contradict this statement but sharpens its focus. The seed of friendship is already there when we encounter a stranger and see Christ in that person. Friendship takes root when the stranger is invited to become a guest. As we come to know our guest, we begin to see all that is good in that person. Yet, we recognize that the source of this goodness, just as of every good thing, is Jesus Christ. Friendship blossoms when we risk opening our lives to one another. Through all the discoveries we then share together, Jesus remains the basis of our love for each other, the center of our relationship.

How do we cultivate Christ-centered friendships? We begin by creating a hospitable space. We make room first in our homes and then in our lives for those who once were no more than strangers to us. Strangers can only be received if we accept them as guests, however. So the second step is that we accept people not for who we wish them to be, but for who they are right now. Finally, we begin to move from the roles of host and guest to the more intimate and honest relationship of true friends. In the words of modern technology, we reach a place of openness by becoming increasingly transparent with each other.

MAKING ROOM

"Hospitality means inviting the stranger into our private space, whether that be the space of our own home or the space of our personal awareness and concern."

Parker Palmer

For many of us, the first step is the toughest: How do we find the time and energy to invite people into our homes and our lives? We began this chapter with the recognition that we face challenges—long working hours, hectic schedules, anonymous suburbs—that previous generations did not have to worry about. Yet, it is also true that making space for others has never been easy.

In the New Testament Book of Hebrews, a Christian leader admonishes members of a congregation by saying, "Let us consider how we may spur one another on toward love and good deeds, not giving up meeting together, as some are in the habit of doing, but encouraging one another" (Hebrews 10:24-25). Apparently, many people had stopped getting together because it was just too difficult. The writer of Hebrews, however, does not let the members of this community off the hook. He reminds them that unless they find time to be with each other, they will not have the resources they need to live a good life. A life of "love and good deeds" requires encouragement, he says. We need each other to spur us along as we follow Jesus.

The message is clear: We need each other in our lives. Together we are more than we can be on our own. Followers of Jesus operate in a similar way to geese flying in a flock. One goose leads the way. The leader cuts the air and makes flying easier for all the geese that follow. The trailing geese take turns crying out to encourage the leader. When the lead goose tires, the leader simply drops back into line and another goose takes the point. If a goose becomes injured and goes to the ground, a second goose will descend and stay by its side. Later, the two of them will join another flock. As followers of Jesus Christ, sometimes we lead, sometimes we follow. Sometimes we are hurting, sometimes we provide care. Yet, in all these situations, we need others by our side. This recognition, according to the author of Hebrews, may be enough to inspire us to gather even when we do not feel like doing so.

Of course, even when we see the importance of getting together, there remains another barrier to hospitality. Most of the time, we just do not feel ready for guests. In her book *Mudhouse Sabbath,* Lauren Winner describes how she struggles to overcome this hurdle:

> Let's consider . . . the seemingly innocent insistence that my apartment is never tidy enough for guests. Well, now. I probably shouldn't have curdling milk in the fridge if I'm inviting someone over for tea, and it might be nice if I emptied the kitchen trash can and didn't leave dirty clothes all over the bathroom floor. But to be a hostess . . . I will have to set down my pride and invite people over even if I have not dusted. . . . If I wait for immaculate, I will never have a guest. . . . Having guests . . . is not an imposition, because we are not meant to rearrange our lives for our guests—we are meant to invite our guests to enter into our lives as they are. It is this forging of relationships that transforms entertaining (i.e. deadly dull cocktail parties at the country club) into hospitality (i.e. a simple pizza on the floor.)[5]

There are all kinds of ways to be a host. We can meet at a coffee shop or call someone to share a workout at the gym. Better still, we can follow Lauren Winner's advice and take the risk to invite people over even when we do not feel prepared. The point, after all, is not to impress, but to open our lives to each other; to create opportunities for encouragement; and to spur each other along as followers of Jesus.

ACCEPTANCE

Mark recalls:

> I once served on the pastoral staff of a large church in Charlotte, North Carolina. I was leaving my office one evening as the Alcoholics Anonymous meeting was about to adjourn. I noticed a man crouched over the hood of a rusty car. I walked over and introduced myself as one of the pastors. He sighed and told me how long he had intended "to get back to church." I invited him to join us for worship. Oddly, his face flushed when I said this; and he immediately launched into the story of his life. It was the familiar string of loss and regret that accompanies addiction. We talked a while longer, shared a prayer, and said good night. As I was walking to my car, he called

> after me. There was urgency in his voice. "Did you mean what you said?" Confused, I asked, "About what?" "Did you really mean that I could come to this church?"
>
> Driving home, it occurred to me why he had told me his life's story. It was a response to my invitation, his polite way of explaining why he could not take me up on my offer. He was trying to tell me that he did not feel good enough about himself to join us. He was suggesting that he had to get it all together before he could come to church.

Why did this man feel more comfortable at Alcoholics Anonymous than at church? Perhaps there was a stronger feeling of mutual acceptance. Folks in AA do not say to the addicted person, "Change and we will accept you." Rather, they say, "Welcome to the club, my friend; we all have the same problem." This is what we long to say to one another in church as well. The Bible reminds us that all of us have fallen short of God's plan for our lives. We all are in the same club. We need God's grace, and we need each other. We know this, but sometimes we need to say it more clearly.

This is the advice Paul often gave to early Christians. In Romans he says, "Honor one another above yourselves" (12:10). In Philippians he sets an even higher standard: "Value others above yourselves" (2:3). In First Thessalonians, Paul gives the strongest encouragement of all: "Now about your love for one another we do not need to write to you, for you yourselves have been taught by God to love each other. And in fact, you do love all the brothers and sisters throughout Macedonia. Yet we urge you, dear friends, to do so more and more" (4:9-10). However much acceptance we show one another, we should always strive to show more. We are never satisfied when it comes to love. We are always on the way to becoming a community of the warm hearth, where love and acceptance shine through all our interactions.

TRANSPARENCY

Once we can trust that we are accepted for who we are, we can really begin to open our lives to each other. We can dare to be honest and transparent in our relationships. But we must be intentional about this. In the eighteenth century, English Methodists gathered in small group meetings. Their goal was to be more transparent with each other. They shared intimately and held one another mutually accountable to continue to grow in Christ. Using their example, one of the best ways to cultivate friendships is to join a small group at a church, where individuals covenant with one another to share their lives openly.

Another way to cultivate friendships is simply to look for those occasions when we can choose to be transparent. Lauren Winner shares a wonderful example of such a moment after she had recently become engaged:

> Griff and I were at a New Year's party, attended, it seemed, by just about everyone we knew. . . . At one point, a curvy red-headed twenty-year old, who happened to have known Griff for a million years and who happened also to be my student, threw herself off the dance floor and into Griff's arms for an entirely innocent and very twenty-year-old-appropriate New Year's hug.
>
> The next week I was chatting about some school matter with the redhead (let's call her Rita Hayworth). I was in mature, collected, professional mode . . . and was not expecting Rita to ask, sweetly, if I had felt uncomfortable about The Hug. I wanted to sound like a grown-up. I wanted to blandly laugh and say, "No, not at all, don't be ridiculous." But some instinct told me to risk transparency with Rita H., that if I couldn't tell her the faintly lame and faintly embarrassing truth about my silly, sad emotions, how was I ever going to be able to tell the truth about something big? So I tried. I told her that actually, when she took that flying dance floor leap into Griff, I felt old and uncool and insecure, . . . and had wanted to kill them both. This truth-telling, to be sure, didn't change the world but it did push me and Rita a bit closer to real knowledge of one another.[6]

When we can learn to be transparent with each other in big and small ways, we experience an intimacy that unites us as one. Christians of an earlier age called such deep hospitality *concordia*. Both Andy and Mark have served as pastors of congregations in a North Carolina town called Concord. It was settled in the eighteenth century by Presbyterian settlers from Scotland and Lutheran settlers from Germany. Each group settled in its own section. They decided to form one town. They called it Concord because *concordia* means a union of hearts. The growth of the town reflected what mature Christian friendships can show: Two or more people become so transparent with each other, sharing a deep mutual acceptance, that there is a union of hearts. It is a union that would have been impossible without the power of the Holy Spirit.

LEARNING TO BE A GUEST

Christian hospitality calls us outward to a place where a genuine sharing of lives can take place. It is an invitation to be both host and guest. For some of us this can be difficult to accept. Some of us find it quite natural to host others, giving our attention, acceptance, and love, but become very uncomfortable when it is our turn to be the guest. As followers of Jesus, we are called both to invite others in and to venture out, sharing our lives with those who welcome us. As we experience together the fire of hospitality, serving as hosts and receiving as guests, we discover that there is always room for one more around the hearth.

"Sometimes your family is the one you make for yourself."
Sarah Jessica Parker

Mark recalls an experience when he felt transformed by the gentle yet persistent hospitality of a fellow Christian:

The summer before I entered seminary, I was a student pastor in a small church of a struggling community of dead and dying tobacco farms. I lived in a little white house with a small screened porch off to the side. Across the street was a woman in her late eighties. Mrs. Mills did not attend our church. She was Baptist; and besides, she did not get out much anymore. She lived alone, homebound in her singlewide trailer; as far as I could tell, she ate every meal alone. Most nights I ate alone too—usually some overcooked meal out of a can. After dinner, I would wave to Mrs. Mills as I began my evening walk. I would pace around those tobacco fields, wondering how it could be that in just three weeks I had gone from an undergraduate with something of a social life to an ill-equipped pastor out in the sticks.

One summer evening, after one of my self-pitying walks, Mrs. Mills knocked on my screen door. She was holding a fried pie, the kind that come individually wrapped from a convenience store. "I thought you might want a little dessert," she said. With some coaxing I convinced her to join me; and somehow by the grace of God I was able to find two clean forks in the kitchen. The next night Mrs. Mills showed up with a handful of powdered doughnuts.

This became our nightly routine throughout that long, hot August. We would talk about our families, about the pains in her sciatica, and about my hopes and dreams for ministry. One night, near the time when I was scheduled to leave and begin seminary, Mrs. Mills knocked on the door holding four vanilla wafers—three for me and one for her. I was ready with two glasses of milk. Mrs. Mills seemed to have something on her mind, so we did not say much. We just shared our dessert together. As I chewed my second stale vanilla wafer, I wondered if she had purchased that box of cookies back in 1973. But I kept that question to myself, and we sat there eating and listening to the sound of the katydids. Finally Mrs. Mills broke the silence. "Mark," she said, "how would it be if from now on you just called me Granny?" Until that moment, I never noticed how much stale vanilla wafers taste like Communion wafers. I never realized that receiving a simple act of hospitality can be as sacred a moment as anything that happens in worship.

---

1. From *Love Feast,* by Frederick Buechner (Scribner, 1974); page 56.
2. From "Nomads," lyrics and music by Carrie Newcomer. Produced by Michael Graham and Robert Meitus (BMI, 1995).
3. From *Love Feast,* by Frederick Buechner; page 56.
4. From *Testimony,* by Tom Long (Jossey-Bass, 2004); page 81.
5. From *Mudhouse Sabbath,* by Lauren Winner (Paraclete Press, 2003); pages 49–50.
6. From *Mudhouse Sabbath,* by Lauren Winner; pages 51–53.

Nine:
How Can We Get Along When We Are So Different?

Conflict Resolution

"What we've got here is failure to communicate."
Prison Camp Superintendent in Cool Hand Luke

"They ate their food with joy and thanksgiving, praising God and showing kindness to everyone."
(Acts 2:46c-47a, authors' paraphrase)

"Certain individuals came down from Judea to Antioch and were teaching the believers: 'Unless you are circumcised, according to the custom taught by Moses, you cannot be saved.' This brought Paul and Barnabas into sharp dispute and debate with them. So Paul and Barnabas were appointed, along with some other believers, to go up to Jerusalem to see the apostles and elders about this question."
(Acts 15:1-2)

CHRISTIAN CONFLICT

Conflict is a fact of life. Whenever two or more people come together in the same room, the same family, or the same congregation, there will always be more than one point of view and certainly more than one opinion. People who are consumed with the passion of Pentecost sometimes burn so strongly that the fire leaps out of the hearth and out of control, leaving only ashes behind. What happens when our experiences and beliefs clash with the experiences and beliefs of another follower of Jesus Christ, or with the Christian community of which we are a part?

One traditional image of the church has sometimes been that of Noah's ark. The Bible tells us that this great vessel saved Noah's family and a multitude of animals from the great Flood (Genesis 6–9). Noah's story has inspired wonderful art and a celebration of the diversity of life and reminds us of God's rainbow of love. Picturing the church as an ark may help us overcome the floods of life. But can you imagine living on an enclosed cargo ship with a dozen close relatives and tens of thousands of animals? The smell, the noise, the constant work, and the inevitable squabbles must have made life together miserable for all the inhabitants. People and animals probably could not wait to abandon the ark as soon as dry land appeared. At times, because the church seems to be like a cluttered and conflicted ark, people may wish to jump ship.

> *"We admit that our community life has included pettiness, insensitivity, harsh judgments, and irresponsibility. We have spoken when we might better have been silent, and we have been silent when we might better have spoken. We have left things to God when we could have helped, and we have tried to do it all ourselves when we could have turned to God."*
>
> *Beth Bussiere-Nichols*

Let us be clear. Even if every Christian in every congregation practiced all the qualities of Christian life we have discussed in this study—being baptized, sharing at table together, praying with one another, watching for signs of God's presence, practicing faithful stewardship, worshiping together, and being hospitable—conflict would occur and might threaten to undo all the good being done. To be the community of Jesus Christ, we must not only practice all the above; we must also learn Christian skills of conflict resolution.

Conflict may be as troublesome as a stone in a shoe, as severe as cancer, as feisty as a fight between a dog and cat, as controversial as a courtroom showdown, or as consuming as a black hole. Conflicts between Christians can arise over a word spoken or a word not spoken, after an action taken or an action not taken, or simply because of differing personalities.

Within Christian congregations, conflicts may occur over many issues: the style of worship, the heat in the sanctuary, the role of women, the color of the carpet, the teacher of a class, the size of the budget. Conflicts can erupt over a theological position, a political topic, an interpretation of Scripture, the church staff, reactions to new members and new perspectives, the pastor's sermon, justice issues in the local community, or social issues that affect the entire world. Congregational conflicts that begin in private may continue in committee meetings, be discussed in the back hallways and parking lot, and be carried forward through e-mails or letters to the local newspaper.

To complicate these points of conflict, many congregations include troublesome people who intensify such struggles: aggressive bullies, constant complainers, negativists, and know-it-alls, as well as others who are silent, unresponsive, indecisive, or too agreeable. We may find in our congregation backbiters who conduct whispering campaigns, autocrats who wish to rule the roost, competitors who want to win at any cost, dependent people who burden the community with their own needs, and stars who need to be the center of attention. Thus, many persons might agree with Marcellinus, a Roman historian in the fourth century: "No wild beasts are so cruel as the Christians in their dealings with each other."[1] Many people might even agree with the old adage, "There are no problems in this congregation that a few Christian funerals would not solve."

"In true community we will not choose our companions, for our choices are so often limited by self-serving motives. Instead, our companions will be given to us by grace. Often

they will be persons who will upset our settled view of self and world. In fact, we might define true community as that place where the person you least want to live with lives!"

Parker Palmer

When basic tensions arise and are made more complicated by troublesome people, conflict spreads. It can be like a computer virus, infecting every computer in the network. A disagreement between two brothers in one congregation can broaden until every member of the congregation has taken a side. When these struggles become destructive, they spiral out of control, spreading to every nook and cranny of a congregation and to all the people within it.

When such "viruses" hit the Christian community, we need a debugging program. If we do not respond appropriately as conflicts escalate and people take sides and establish positions, many other people will move to the sidelines or out the exit gates. Well-intentioned church members may end up exhausted and wounded physically, emotionally, and spiritually.

FRICTION IN THE CHURCH

One way to envision conflict in our lives and in Christian community comes from Andy's experience with his knees:

> During college, I injured my knees playing soccer. At that time, the consensus of my physicians was that I should learn to live with the damage. For almost thirty years, my knees hurt. When I walked, ran, or played sports, I could feel the bones in my knees rubbing against each another. The pain was chronic and sometimes sharp. Rob Weber suggested glucosamine and chondroitin sulfate, but they did not work. Finally, after three decades of pain, I went to a new doctor with new surgical techniques. Two weeks later, he performed outpatient surgery on my most troublesome knee. When I awoke, I could tell immediately that the pain was gone. No longer did I feel the grinding together of my bones.

Should we simply tolerate friction in the church or seek to heal it? The answer is obvious.

Another way to envision conflict involves our image of the church as the body of Christ (1 Corinthians 12:12-31). When the parts of the body—foot, hand, ear, eye—all work together, the body is healthy. But when the parts of the body work against each other, as with Andy's knees, the pain is real. The foot bone may grind against the leg bone, against the hipbone, against the backbone, against the neck bone; and the pain increases. As it does, our spirits tense up, our speech becomes muddled, and our hearing is impaired. We can put off surgery; but if we want to feel good again, we cannot avoid dealing with the problem forever.

> *"As long as we are on earth, the love that unites us will bring us suffering by our very contact with one another, because this love is the resetting of a Body of broken bones. Even saints cannot live with saints on this earth without some anguish, without some pain at the differences that come between them. There are two things [people] can do about the pain of disunion with other [people]. They can love or they can hate."*
>
> *Thomas Merton*

HOW DO WE RESPOND TO CONFLICT?

How should Christians respond to conflict? Some of our responses occur at a subliminal level. For example, in a time of disagreement we may experience a knot in our stomach when a certain person enters the room. A nagging issue results in our tossing and turning in bed throughout a sleepless night. We might even fear walking into the church. As the conflict grows, we may fight or flee or sue or be sued.

How do we engage in conflicts in our personal lives and in the church in ways that build us up rather than tear us down? We cannot choose our conflicts. We can choose, however, how to respond when problems divide us from one another. We have a number of options as we respond to conflict. In a particular situation, there may be more than one Christian way to respond to it.

Some responses to conflict seem to add to the problem rather than resolve it. For example, denial or avoidance moves us around a problem and prevents us from dealing with the source of the conflict, allowing the problem to fester. We might point the finger, naming a particular person as the source of the problem, which often results in fingers being pointed at us. Or we might respond to conflict with anger and lash out, a response that, though sometimes useful, may cut off all possibility of conflict resolution.

Better options for conflict resolution are available to us. Accommodation involves adjusting our beliefs or actions to suit the other, graciously making room for everybody at the table. Compromise means listening, negotiating, and holding one another to a mutually agreed upon solution in a give-and-take dialogue. Collaboration engages the whole congregation in living and working together; as one author wrote, collaboration involves "a trustworthy environment where all are informed, communication is open, and each person has fair opportunity to influence the outcome."[2] Each conflict may require a different strategy or several of these strategies for resolution.

No one response to conflict is best; all of them point to a common goal. Beyond conflict we may discover God's profound desire for reconciliation among all people—with God, with one another, and with creation. We may learn how to listen to one another, speak calmly, fight fairly, challenge appropriately, respect one another, and learn skills that assist us in every aspect of our lives. The Bible begins by reminding us that God creates order out of chaos (Genesis 1). We cannot eliminate conflict, but we can learn how to resolve it.

"Through all members of the Body working together, even, maybe particularly, through conflict, the Body is strengthened."

Norma Cook Everist

JESUS CHRIST AND CONFLICT

Jesus himself understood conflict. The brute force of Roman occupiers dominated first-century Palestine. The Jewish people divided themselves into a wide variety of sects with differing political and religious agendas, and Jesus' teaching created conflict between him and some of the religious authorities. Jesus' own death resulted from his conflict with the political and religious authorities. Yet, violent conflict did not end Jesus' story. Beyond the accusations, trial, and crucifixion, resurrection and life triumphed!

Jesus gave us a number of illustrations of how to respond to conflict. For example, Jesus told us:

> "Love one another. As I have loved you, so you must love one another."
>
> (John 13:34)

> "Blessed are the peacemakers,
> for they will be called children of God."
> (Matthew 5:9)

> "You have heard that it was said to the people long ago, 'You shall not murder, and anyone who murders will be subject to judgment.' But I tell you that anyone who is angry with a brother or sister will be subject to judgment. . . . Therefore, if you are offering your gift at the altar and there remember that your brother or sister has something against you, leave your

> gift there in front of the altar. First go and be reconciled to that person; then come and offer your gift."
>
> (Matthew 5:21-24)

> "You have heard that it was said, 'Love your neighbor and hate your enemy.' But I tell you, love your enemies and pray for those who persecute you, that you may be children of your Father in heaven."
>
> (Matthew 5:43-45)

> "If a brother or sister sins, go and point out the fault, just between the two of you. If they listen to you, you have won them over. But if they will not listen, take one or two others along, so that 'every matter may be established by the testimony of two or three witnesses.' If they refuse to listen, tell it to the church; and if they refuse to listen even to the church, treat them as you would a pagan or a tax collector."
>
> (Matthew 18:15-17)

These words from Jesus often challenged the early church; and they still challenge us today, even as they give us comfort in dealing with conflict.

CONFLICT AMONG THE FIRST CHRISTIANS

While the disciples on the Day of Pentecost appeared to have triumphed over all their initial controversies among themselves, the rest of the Acts of the Apostles reveals over and over again that there were individual disagreements, congregational strife, and conflicts with authorities. The church was born and bred amidst conflict.

The first major battle in the post-Pentecost church occurred between Jewish Christians and Gentile Christians (Acts 15). Paul, who had spent much of his ministry bringing Gentiles (anyone who was not Jewish) into the church, traveled with some friends to Jerusalem in about the year 48. There he had a face-to-face encounter with the first disciples, who had remained in Jerusalem to encourage Jews to accept Jesus as the Messiah. At issue was whether Gentiles should become Jewish and obey Jewish practices before they became Christians or Gentiles could become followers of Christ without first being Jews. Everyone had staked out a position and was ready to defend it. The conflict could have killed the growing church, leaving it in the ashes of history.

> *"It is not in differing from one another that disunity arises—it is in not listening to God and each other."*
>
> *Kenneth Sutton*

Instead, Paul and Peter, the Jews and the Gentiles, the long-time disciples and the new converts, began to talk. They remembered to speak with, not to or at, one another. Paul described everything that God was doing in his mission to the Gentiles. Peter described his own visions from God. Together they read the Scriptures and prayed. Together they asked the Holy Spirit to guide them in what to do. Rather than continuing to fight with one another, the whole community asked what God wanted them to do. Then they listened for a word from God. At the end of their conversation, they reached a decision. The Jewish Christians declared, "We should not make it difficult for the Gentiles who are turning to God" (Acts 15:19). Both Jews and Gentiles would be welcomed in God's holy church. The Jerusalem Conference set a pattern for conflict resolution that we can follow today.

> *"Living the spiritual life means living life as one unified reality. The forces of darkness are the forces that split, divide, and set in opposition. The forces of light unite. Literally, the word 'diabolic' means dividing. The demon divides; the Spirit unites."*
>
> *Henri Nouwen*

MOVING FROM CONFLICT TO RESOLUTION

"All of us . . . are diminished and dishonored when we do not meet each other halfway. How can we love in truth and lovingly help one another in this? Because we must remember that truth without love is violence. And love without truth is sentimentality. We do need both."

Muriel Bishop

Sometimes we may have to acknowledge that we, not others, are the source of the problem. One day a man was driving through an unfamiliar neighborhood. As he drove along, people began yelling at him. The driver locked his doors and kept driving. As he continued down the road, people screamed at him and used a variety of gestures to get his attention. The driver thought, *Those rude people!* He rolled up his windows and turned up the radio to drown out all their cries. What was wrong with all those jerks? The driver got angrier and angrier, blowing his horn at the people and gesturing back to them. Then, all of a sudden, the driver realized that he was driving the wrong way down a one-way street. Sometimes other people are not the problem; sometimes we are the problem.

"To get rid of an enemy, one must love him."

Leo Tolstoy

Musicians playing together illustrate Christians working together at their best. A choir takes very different voices—sopranos, altos, tenors, and basses—and merges their tones and ranges into one harmonic unity. The issue is not whether one person or section is superior or louder or more tuneful than the other. The best choirs are not necessarily those with the best voices but those choirs that best blend the voices together. Likewise, the best orchestras are not those with the best individual instrumentalists or the best musical sections. The best orchestras merge the various musicians and instruments into one body to make one unified sound.

HOW ARE WE TO RESOLVE CONFLICT?

The Mennonites, a Christian denomination known for their efforts to live in peace, have adopted guidelines to help individuals and congregations deal with conflict. "Agreeing and Disagreeing in Love: Commitments for Mennonites in Times of Disagreement" is based on principles discovered and practiced by the early church. Exceptionally comprehensive and helpful, this Mennonite document states:

> Making every effort to maintain the unity of the Spirit in the bond of peace . . . , as both individual members and the body of Christ, we pledge that we shall:
>
> *In Thought*
> 1. Accept conflict: Acknowledge together that conflict is a normal part of our life in the church. . . .
> 2. Affirm hope: Affirm that as God walks with us in conflict we can work through [it] to growth. . . .
> 3. Commit to prayer: Admit our needs and commit ourselves to pray for a mutually satisfactory solution . . . .
>
> *In Action*
> 4. Go to the other. . . : Go directly to those with whom we disagree. . . .
> 5. Go in gentleness, patience, and humility. . . .
> 6. Be quick to listen. . . .
> 7. Be slow to judge. . . .
> 8. Be willing to negotiate. . . .
>
> *In Life*
> 9. Be steadfast in love. . . .
> 10. Be open to mediation. . . .
> 11. Trust the community. . . .
> 12. Be the body of Christ: Believe in and rely on the solidarity of the body of Christ and its commitment to peace and justice.[3]

"Civility does not mean the mere outward gentleness of speech cultivated for the occasion, but an inborn gentleness and desire to do the opponent good."

Mohandas Gandhi

In 1993, sworn enemies Yitzhak Rabin (Prime Minister of Israel) and Yasser Arafat (leader of the Palestine Liberation Organization) stood together on the lawn of the White House with President Bill Clinton. Rabin and Arafat met to give their assent to a peace plan between their two peoples. Each man had been sharply criticized by segments of his own people for meeting with the enemy and formally recognizing the other side. Facing the criticism, Prime Minister Rabin observed, "You don't make peace with your friends; you make peace with your enemies."[4]

LIFE BEYOND CONFLICT

When we recognize our common humanity and our need for resolution even in the face of disagreement, conflict may be resolved. Such resolution is required in organizations and in our daily lives. When organizations seek vision for their future, one technique they can use is called Affirmative Inquiry. Affirmative Inquiry requires that before we move forward, we must remember and celebrate our shared history and values. We can only move forward when we remember our past connections and successes.

The need for Affirmative Inquiry also exists in smaller settings. In the classic movie T*o Kill a Mockingbird,* lawyer Atticus Finch defended an African American man accused of raping a white woman. Everyone involved in the story was a Christian. One night, Atticus sat in front of the courthouse jail to prevent the lynching of his client. An angry white crowd gathered in front of Atticus. As the tension increased, Atticus' two children, Jem and Scout, appeared and stood beside their father. Atticus was worried about the safety of his children and urged them to return home, but the children remained for the sake of their father. As they stood together, his daughter, Scout, scanned the crowd, recognized a leader of the mob, and spoke:

"Hey, Mr. Cunningham. Don't you remember me, Mr. Cunningham? I'm Jean Louise Finch. You brought us some hickory nuts early one morning, remember? We had a talk. I went and got my daddy to come out and thank you. I go to school with your boy. I go to school with Walter. He's a nice boy. Tell him 'hey' for me, won't you?"

Silence engulfed the angry crowd. Everyone watched Scout and Mr. Cunningham. A conversation had begun. How would it end? Scout sensed a change in the atmosphere and spoke again: "What's the matter? I sure meant no harm, Mr. Cunningham." The silence continued.

Then Cunningham, the leader of the mob, replied, "No harm taken, young lady." Cunningham bent down to Scout's level, held her shoulders, and said, "I'll tell Walter you said 'hey,' little lady." Cunningham then turned to disperse the angry men: "Let's clear outta here. Let's go, boys."[5] Shared memories and relationships, maybe even the presence of our reconciling God, turned violence into peace.

"Love one another and do not strive for another's undoing."
Seneca Proverb

LIVING IN PEACE

Belonging to one another, experiencing community with one another, and being a part of the church brings together people with differing perspectives and a diversity of values. In a book on conflict in congregations, the author quotes a young woman named Rose: "We were created together for communion with God and one another as we celebrate and struggle for unity and our diversity. Conflict and collaboration are integral components of this celebration and struggle. We rejoice, dance, eat together, question, agree, disagree, challenge, and embrace. We learn. We grow. God is faithful in meeting us during the times of peace and tranquility and in times of anger, frustration, and disparity. God is faithful in the very messiness of our lives."[6]

What would peaceful resolution of our conflicts look like in our personal lives and in our Christian communities? Husbands and wives would listen more carefully to each other and ask not "What do I want?" but "What does our marriage need?" Parents and children would listen to one another and ask not "What can I get out of this family?" but "How can we grow together?" Workers and bosses would work together instead of against one another. Friends would stop talking and start listening and then put their friendship first instead of their own needs. Members of a congregation would work together for the good of the whole.

> *"Love interrupts, if you like, the consequences of your actions, which in my case is very good news indeed, because I've done a lot of stupid stuff."*
>
> *Bono*

Andy remembers how a wise man taught him to resolve a divisive conflict in his local congregation:

> Our church was trying to decide whether to begin a daycare program in our new facility. Some members wanted daycare as a Christian alternative for our younger members and new residents in our community. Other members wondered about the likely damage to the building and the initial expenses. Many questions arose. We debated the issue over several months at a variety of congregational meetings. We prayed often and kept lines of communication open. Several members threatened to leave the congregation if their position failed to win.

At our final meeting on the issue, the church board debated again for over an hour. The conversation was tense but civil. People said what they believed but then listened to other people speak. We took several minutes for silent prayer. Then we voted by secret ballot. The decision was to proceed with daycare. But it was not unanimous. Would schism follow?

After the vote was announced, Dale, one of the board members whose position did not prevail, addressed the group. Dale said that although he disagreed with the decision, for the sake of the congregation the board members must leave the meeting united. Dale declared that he would publicly be supportive, and then he called for a second vote. The second vote was unanimous. This man, who had lost the vote, did not become a loser. Dale built a bridge, not a wall. That board meeting felt to me like the Jerusalem Conference all over again.

---

1. From *Never Call Them Jerks,* by Arthur Boers (Alban Institute, 1999); page 1.
2. From *Church Conflict: From Contention to Collaboration*, by Norma Cook Everist (Abingdon Press, 2004); page 149.
3. From "Agreeing and Disagreeing in Love: Commitments for Mennonites in Times of Disagreement" (1995). For further information, contact the Peace and Justice Committee, Mennonite Church, P.O. Box 173, Orrville, Ohio 44667.
4. From *Making Peace With Conflict,* by Dean Peachey (Herald Press, 1999); page 94.
5. From *To Kill a Mockingbird,* by Harper Lee (Lippincott, 1960). Sceenplay by Horton Foote (1962).
6. From *Church Conflict: From Contention to Collaboration,* by Norma Cook Everist; page 12.

Ten:
How Do We Share What We Have Discovered?

Witness

"Evangelism is witness. It is one beggar telling another beggar where to get food. Christians do not offer out of their bounty. They have no bounty. They are simply guests at their Master's table and, as evangelists, they call others too."

Bishop D. T. Niles

"And day by day, the Lord God increased the number of persons who were being saved."

(Acts 2:47b, authors' paraphrase)

"While Paul was waiting for [Silas and Timothy] in Athens, he was greatly distressed to see that the city was full of idols. So he reasoned in the synagogue with both Jews and God-fearing Greeks, as well as in the marketplace day by day with those who happened to be there. A group of Epicurean and Stoic philosophers began to debate with him.... Then they took him ... to a meeting of the Areopagus, where they said to him, 'May we know what this new teaching is that you are presenting? You are bringing some strange ideas to our ears, and we would like to know what they mean.' ...

"When they heard about the resurrection of the dead, some of them sneered, but others said, 'We want to hear you again on this subject.' At that, Paul left the Council. Some of the people became followers of Paul and believed."

(Acts 17:16-34)

SHARING THE BANQUET

In C. S. Lewis' *The Lion, the Witch, and the Wardrobe*, a young girl named Lucy discovered a new world called Narnia. Lucy had stumbled into Narnia through an ordinary-looking wardrobe and found a land of fawns, witches, and talking animals. When Lucy returned home, she told her story to her three siblings. As the tale continues:

> Lucy ran out of the empty room into the passage and found the other three.
>
> "It's all right," she reported, "I've come back."
>
> "What on earth are you talking about, Lucy?" asked Susan. . . .
>
> "I've been away for hours and hours, and had tea, and all sorts of things have happened."
>
> "Don't be silly, Lucy," said Susan. . . .
>
> "She's not being silly at all," said Peter, "she's just making up a story for fun."
>
> "No, Peter, I'm not," she said. "It's—a magic wardrobe. There's a wood inside it, and it's snowing, and there's a faun and a witch and it's called Narnia; come and see."
>
> The others did not know what to think.[1]

Lucy had walked into a new reality. She could not wait to tell about it. Yet, as she discovered, not everyone wanted to listen.

When we have experienced a living relationship with Jesus Christ and understand the power of Christian community, our natural instinct calls us to tell other people what we have discovered. Imagine how our lives would be different if somebody—our parents, our grandparents, a school friend, a neighbor, a coworker—had not invited us to God's banquet. Sharing the good news of Jesus Christ with hungry people is both a personal opportunity for individual believers and the Christ-given mission of every congregation. The followers of Jesus Christ from the Day of Pentecost to the present day form a community of storytellers, people who faithfully and truthfully can witness about Jesus Christ.

Most of us remember who first told us about Jesus: a grandparent reading a Bible story, a parent saying a prayer at night, a teacher at school or Sunday school describing a better way, a friend who expressed an interest in us, a mentor who shared the meaning of life. Biblical scholar James Saunders dedicated one of his books to "Sisters Agnes and Iris and my sister, Nell, women who told me the tomb was empty, and Ruth and Joe Brown Love, who told me my head need not be."[2] In every case, a follower of Jesus Christ took the time to pull us aside from the busyness of life and speak to us about God.

We believe that people are hungry for true God-talk: our intimate sharing with another person about how God works in our lives. The words they long to hear are healing words, comforting words, nurturing words, and saving words. We all have experiences with God that we yearn to share. When we learn to witness, we transform other people and discover more about our own faith. We may already be in a relationship with another person, but speaking the words *I love you* forever changes that relationship. If we are silent, we miss the opportunity. We have the same opportunity in speaking about our love of God and neighbor.

> *"A healthy church is one in which we seek to stay connected with God by seeking to connect others with God.... A church that is living in such a way is the only church that will have anything different to say to the world."*
>
> *Rowan Williams*

SHARE THE STORY

When we have found community with other people and with God, we yearn for other people to discover it, too. Three words give focus to this aspect of living together in community.

The word *evangelism* comes from the Greek *euangelion,* meaning "good news" or "gospel." Through evangelism we share with other people the good news of Jesus Christ; we point out Jesus to friends, neighbors, and coworkers. Yet, this word is associated with negative experiences for some people; and many Christians shy away from this language.

Two other biblical words may open new possibilities for us: *testimony* and *witness*. These words come from the world of law. When somebody is on trial, a witness gives testimony about what she or he knows is true. The role of the witness is not to ask questions or to render final judgment. Instead, the witness responds to questions from inquirers on all sides and speaks truthfully about what has been seen or experienced. As we remember from courtroom dramas on television, witnesses are "to tell the truth, the whole truth, and nothing but the truth, so help me God."

> *"While we chatter or listen all our lives in a din of craving—jokes, anecdotes, novels, dreams, films, plays, songs, half the words of our days—we are satisfied only by the one short tale we feel to be true: History is the will of a just God who knows us."*
>
> *Reynolds Price*

FAILING TO WITNESS

Unfortunately, too many followers of Jesus Christ have forgotten to tell the story or are fearful of being a witness. We may begin to act as if the banquet is only for us. We may live as if the church were a private club; if people want to join, they must come to us, follow our rules, and be voted into the club. At the other end of the spectrum, we agonize that if we talk about God in the wrong place, we will never again be invited out to lunch or to a party. We may begin to fear that if we open the table to other people, there may not be enough food to satisfy our own hunger. We may assume that people do not want to hear what we have to say. We are uncertain about which words we are to use. We fear that the task is too large. Which of us really believes that we alone can make "disciples of all nations" (Matthew 28:19)? For many reasons, we shy away from being faithful witnesses.

> *"I'm a Jehovah's Bystander. [We're] like the Witnesses, only we don't want to get involved."*
>
> *Flip Wilson*

In "The Burning" episode of the television show *Seinfeld*, Elaine suspects that her boyfriend Puddy is a Christian. Elaine discovers this truth when she borrows Puddy's car and learns that her boyfriend has tuned the radio to a Christian radio station. Elaine, in anger, pries a "Jesus fish" off her friend's bumper. She becomes mad at Puddy because "he seemed so one-dimensional, I feel misled." When Elaine asks Puddy about his Christian faith, this conversation follows:

Elaine: "Do you believe in God?"
Puddy: "Yes." . . .
Elaine: "So is it a problem that I'm not really religious?"
Puddy: "Not for me."
Elaine: "Why not?"
Puddy: "I'm not the one going to hell."[3]

With typical *Seinfeld* humor, the episode showed that although Elaine had no interest in God or Christianity, she believed that if Puddy really cared about her, he would talk about his faith. Elaine was correct. Puddy, reflecting a shallow understanding of testimony, failed in his task of being a witness.

We also fail to witness when we do so inappropriately. We may not want to be identified with evangelists who walk up and down the aisles of a crowded room, pointing fingers and condemning everyone in sight. The book title *When Bad Christians Happen to Good People* illustrates this fear. In the aftermath of Hurricane Katrina, the people in New Orleans remember vividly the groups of Christians who came to Jackson Square in the center of the city. These Christians arrived with amplifiers and loud speakers, and with in-your-face tactics they proclaimed the hurricane and flood to be the wrath of God upon a sinful city. The actions of these aggressive witnesses drove their listeners further away from God. Such actions also make us leery of wanting the label "witness" for ourselves. Yet, we must be careful not to walk away from opportunities to testify.

"When God is seeking a person, God will not allow my fear, my feeling of intimidation or my lack of knowledge or experience to prevent that person from finding God."

Rebecca Manley Pippert

WITNESSES IN JERUSALEM AND IN ATHENS

The first followers of Jesus Christ offer us a different way of being storytellers, of allowing other people to belong. Think about those first disciples. Peter and John, for example, were uneducated fishermen from the hinterlands of their country. Yet, in the days after Pentecost, when they spoke about their relationship with Jesus Christ, people were "astonished and they took note that these men had been with Jesus" (Acts 4:13). Peter said, "We cannot help speaking about what we have seen and heard" (Acts 4:20).

"The New Testament church engaged in evangelism as naturally and normally as a robin sings or a happy child plays."

Harold DeWolf

In the first days after Pentecost, the new church in Jerusalem grew rapidly. Through the power of the Holy Spirit, thousands of Gentiles and Jews heard the good news of Jesus, offered their lives to the Lord, were baptized and taught by the apostles, shared their property, and went out to tell others the news.

Then a new follower joined their company and expanded the vision of who might be hungry for the good news of Jesus Christ. Paul, a former persecutor of the church, believed that the church could not just stay in Jerusalem but had to spread throughout the world. Paul dedicated his life to taking the good news of Jesus Christ to other peoples and other nations.

> *"The first-generation Christians lived this radical faith every day. Their actions caught the world's attention both positively and negatively, but their actions—like ours—were not calculated to bring a response; rather, their actions and ours are a response. A response to God's amazing grace."*
>
> *Reuben Job*

One day, Paul arrived in Athens, the intellectual center of the Roman Empire and the home of Socrates, Plato, and Aristotle. Athens was the artistic, philosophic, and religious capital of the Greco-Roman world. At the highest point in Athens was the Acropolis, on which stood the great Parthenon; and in the center of the Parthenon stood a forty-foot-tall wooden statue of the goddess Athena, her face and hands made of ivory and her body covered with two hundred fifty pounds of gold. The exterior wall displayed a procession of hundreds of Greek gods. Athens celebrated the fact that there were more statues of gods in Athens than in all the rest of Greece. The Roman satirist Juvenal said, "It is easier to meet a god than a person in Athens."[4]

Just below the Acropolis stood a small hill called the Areopagus, the place of meeting. In this place, overshadowed by idols and looking down on the great schools, Paul declared that the Athenians were looking for God in all the wrong places. He testified before Stoics, Epicureans, Jews, and all who would listen to him about the life, death, and resurrection of Jesus Christ. As this difficult audience listened to Paul's witness, some people "sneered," others wanted "to hear [him] again on this subject" (Acts 17:32), and still others "believed" (Acts 17:34).

> *"The dramatic change in the lives of people touched by the power and presence of God through the early church proved to be a nearly irresistible magnet, drawing many to believe in and follow Jesus Christ.... Today people still look for evidence of God's transforming presence in the church and in the world. When they find that evidence, they often turn toward it."*
>
> *Reuben Job*

WHY DO WE WITNESS?

Why should we be less like Flip Wilson or Puddy and more like Paul? The first and most obvious reason is because Jesus invited us to do so. Just before Jesus ascended to heaven following his resurrection, he instructed his disciples, "Therefore go and make disciples of all nations" (Matthew 28:19). Then, in the Acts of the Apostles, Jesus said, "You will receive power when the Holy Spirit comes on you; and you will be my witnesses in Jerusalem, and in all Judea and Samaria, and to the ends of the earth" (Acts 1:8). Jesus intended that we tell about what we have experienced.

On a personal level, all of us have a basic need to share our experiences with others. Meeting a famous person, eating a great meal, catching a large fish, finding the cheapest gas, purchasing a special piece of clothing—all these experiences cause us to want to share the news. It should not be surprising, then, that when we have found a new life in Jesus Christ, when our hearts and minds and feet have been changed, and when we find a community of love, our experiences draw us out to tell our stories. As God has shared with us, we want to share with others.

WHO IS TO WITNESS?

Many Christians say, "Witnessing is not my job. Testifying is the role of my pastor, or the traveling evangelist, or that small group of people in our congregation who serve on the evangelism committee." The task of sharing does not belong just to church professionals or to a few passionate people, however. Christ invites all of us to witness to other women and men, youth, and children.

Rob once met a man named Bill Moore, who had a depth of passion to testify. When Moore walked into the room, he looked like a rock star from decades ago. Resembling a band member from the group "Deep Purple," Moore had long black hair hanging halfway down his back. Moore served as a pastor in one of the roughest neighborhoods in New York City, a community filled with poverty, addiction, and violence. Moore's ministry focused on using buses to bring children to worship. Moore told Rob this story:

> One day a woman from Puerto Rico started coming to worship. She did not speak English, but she came and came again. Although her life involved drugs and prostitution, she heard the message that Jesus Christ loved her dearly. When she heard this good news, the woman received it with such joy that she immediately began to wonder how to share it. She asked Moore, "How can I give back? I do not have any skills." In response, Moore asked her to assist on one of the buses, just to ride along with the children coming to worship. She accepted his invitation.
>
> One day a new child started to ride the woman's bus. Quiet and withdrawn, the little boy appeared to have had a life filled with pain and abuse. The woman felt drawn to the child. She began to hold him close. He rode in her lap. No matter how closely she held him, he did

> not speak. Finally, she began to tell him the only words she knew in English: "I love you" and "Jesus loves you." She became a witness. That little boy on her lap turned around. His eyes met hers; and he said, "I love you, too." The bus dropped the child off at 2:30 that afternoon. At 6:30 that evening, someone found his body in a dumpster in a garbage bag. His mother had beaten him to death. Yet, Moore proclaimed that he believed that the child, through this woman, knew the love of God.

Like Moore and the Puerto Rican woman, why would we not want to share the good news with other people who are so hungry to hear?

WHEN AND WHERE DO WE WITNESS?

When do we witness? We witness whenever the occasion of a friend in need calls forth our testimony. Where do we witness? We witness everywhere someone needs to hear a good word.

We witness when we greet our families in the morning or pick up children in a carpool, when we have a cup of coffee or tea with our coworkers, when we participate in a business meeting, when we sit at the lunch counter with a friend, as we greet friends at the health club, as we watch a child's sports team with other parents, when we attend a wedding or a funeral. Even children can participate in such witness. In an old joke, a teacher asks a young girl what she is drawing. The child responds, "I am drawing a picture of God." The teacher says, "But no one knows what God looks like." The child replies, "They will when I finish." When we witness, all of us draw such pictures for our friends and family.

> "Always be prepared to give an answer to everyone who asks you to give the reason for the hope that you have. But do this with gentleness and respect."
>
> (1 Peter 3:15)

Alex Mukulu was a Ugandan actor and musician who lived during the brutal regime of Idi Amin. During those years Mukulu worked on a play entitled *The Prince of Peace*. Why? "In our country there was no peace at all," he said. "We were fighting for twenty years. I wanted to create a character who could be a symbol of peace and a model for as many people as we could reach." When Mukulu was working on the play, each day as he walked to work, he observed an old man sitting by a window reading a book. One day Mukulu stopped and spoke with the man. He learned that the old man was reading the Bible. When Mukulu described his play, the old man replied, "You cannot give what you don't have. If you want to give people peace, you need to have peace. The peace you need is the peace of Jesus Christ. If you want this peace, I will pray for you." Mukulu became a Christian missionary to the United States. One old man's witness created a new believer and ultimately a new witness for Jesus Christ.[5] Mukulu responded to Jesus Christ's invitation and offered the invitation to others.

HOW DO WE TELL THE STORY?

How do we talk about God in our everyday lives at home or at work? When we are at dinner parties or at the gym or at the PTA, we seem to be able to talk about politics, sex, money, or anything else—except God. How do we offer God-talk without arrogance, embarrassment, or offense? How can we speak inviting words to our children, our parents, our friends, our coworkers, or our neighbors? People yearn for God-talk, not used as a weapon, but used to transform lives.

At one level, sharing our faith involves being a living witness for Jesus Christ. "Lifestyle evangelism" occurs when other people see our lives in communion with Jesus Christ and want to be like us. The previous chapters of this book indicate a number of ways in which our lives can offer witness about Jesus Christ: when we are washed by water and the Holy Spirit, gather around a table together, pray together, point out God's signs and wonders, share our resources, gather for worship, practice hospitality, become peacemakers. Every time we practice these Christian behaviors, people outside the Christian community watch us and may seek to belong.

> *"Witnessing is not a spare-time occupation or once-a-week activity. It must be a quality of life. You don't go witnessing; you are a witness."*
>
> *Dan Greene*

Besides setting an example, sharing also requires conversation. Sharing is not primarily about saving souls from hell or preserving the institutional church or promoting the program of a congregation. It is neither the annual revival nor completion of a membership class. Sharing is not passing confirmation or distributing a tract or watching a television evangelist or even joining a congregation. Sharing is engaging in human conversation with people who need to talk. [See *Beginnings: An Introduction to Christian Faith,* especially *Along the Way: A Participant's Companion,* by Andy Langford and Mark Ralls (Abingdon Press, 2003); pages 203–205 for some additional ideas about witnessing.]

> *"An invitation binds the inviter and the invitee together in a new way. When an invitation has been issued, there is both a connection and a risk involved. The invitation bonds the two together, no matter what the answer to the invitation."*
>
> *Peggy Way*

Andy's congregation decided to take the gospel out of their church facilities to a local pub. In their small town of Concord, North Carolina, a popular gathering place was the George Washington Tavern. Owned by friends of the church, the tavern featured live music and an expansive bar area. Upstairs, the congregation reserved a meeting room with a smaller bar, tables, pool table, and dartboard. As Andy recalls:

> We decided to offer *Beginnings: An Introduction to Christian Faith* on Tuesday nights. Our congregation provided the appetizers; persons would order their own drinks. Most people drank iced tea (remember, this is the South), and some had beer. A biker joined our conversation, along with a street person and some friends of friends. As we sat around open tables to talk about our own relationship with God, other people joined the circle. For twelve weeks, we gathered over wings and chips, listened to Rob speak on the videos, and discussed the theme of the day. As the class continued, participants invited more friends into the circle. Even our waitress joined in the conversation.

Many opportunities arise in which we may share the love of God: a marriage or divorce, the birth of a child or the death of a loved one, the start of a new job or the unexpected loss of one, an injury or recovery from illness, the beginning of college or retirement, Christmas or Easter, moving to a new town or leaving one's hometown. In these moments and others, we describe how God works in the world; and we speak God's words. We share with others the hope and comfort we find in our relationship with Jesus Christ.

"We are most truly human only when we use words like Jesus used them: to bless and not to curse, to build up and not to tear down, to point to the mystery of God pervading all of life and not to refer only, always, and incessantly to ourselves."
Thomas Long

WITNESSING IN OUR CONGREGATION

"The Church exists for those outside."
William Temple

Our testimony cannot be limited just to one-on-one conversations; our congregation as a whole is also called to witness. For example, how do we welcome visitors? Are we protective of our seats in the sanctuary? Do we talk only with friends? Do we smile, speak, shake hands, or stare? Some years ago, Andy was visiting in Singapore. While there, he visited a number of Hindu and Buddhist places of worship. He recalls:

> The sights, sounds, and smells were quite different from anything I had ever experienced. I had a thousand questions. What was the purpose of the statues, the incense, and the art on the walls? What were the people saying to one another? When was the time of worship? What was expected of me as a visitor? I was terribly frustrated because nobody was available to explain to me what I was seeing and experiencing. As a result, while I found these places of worship interesting, I have no interest in going back.

Many inquirers feel just that way about our congregations. Where do we sit? How should we act? What is expected? What is appropriate? Imagine the difference it would make if someone walked up to the guests; greeted them warmly; and introduced them to the space, the activities, and the people. What we sometimes forget is that many guests perceive our local congregations as alien worlds and cultures, just like Andy's experience in Singapore.

> *"The church is the only institution in the world that exists for the sake of non-members."*
>
> *William Temple*

Henri Nouwen understands this witnessing of the body of Christ as a form of hospitality:

> Hospitality not to change people, but to offer them space where change can take place. It is not to bring men and women over to our side, but to offer freedom not disturbed by dividing lines. It is not to lead our neighbor into a corner where there are no alternatives left, but to open a wide spectrum of options for choice and commitment.

> It is not an educated intimidation with good books, good stories and good works, but the liberation of fearful hearts so that words can find roots and bear simple fruit.[6]

Rob once wrote that our society is full of "tourists" who are not sure what to make of us Christians. These tourists are watching from the balconies of our daily lives. While some of these people look on for entertainment, there are some who long to know if the church has something to offer them. Can Jesus be who we say he is?

Witnessing by the congregation may happen in many ways. Several years ago, a member of Andy's congregation was dying of cancer. He had to remain housebound and could not receive visitors. His wife stayed beside him throughout his struggle, still managing to sing every week in the church choir. Their friends wanted to be supportive but did not know what to do. As Christmas came near and the man's health failed, the choir decided to witness to their support and their faith by going to the couple's home. Outside the front door, the choir began to sing Christmas carols. They sang:

> Hail the heaven-born Prince of Peace!
> Hail the Sun of Righteousness!
> Light and life to all he brings,
> risen with healing in his wings.
> Mild he lay the glory by,
> born that we no more may die,
> born to raise us from the earth,
> born to give us second birth.
> Hark! the herald angels sing,
> "Glory to the new born King!"[7]

The choir's witness brought tears to the eyes of everyone inside and outside that home. When the man died the next day, the choir realized that what they learned in worship they had given witness to on the sidewalk of a neighborhood.

WHAT HAPPENS WHEN WE WITNESS?

When we witness, we cannot always expect the dramatic results of Pentecost, when three thousand new believers joined the church. After all, some people rejected Paul's testimony in Athens, other people wanted to hear more, and only a few became believers. We can never accurately predict the fruits of our labors.

Flannery O'Connor, in her story "A Temple of the Holy Ghost," tells of several young adolescent girls who were instructed in their Roman Catholic school to say, "I am a Temple of the Holy Ghost." For example, Sister Perpetua told the girls that if a young man were to act inappropriately in the back of an automobile, the girls were to say, "I am a Temple of the Holy Ghost." Later in the story, two fourteen-year-old girls laughed when recounting that experience; but a twelve-year-old friend overheard their conversation. When the younger child heard them, she rejoiced. " 'I am a Temple of the Holy Ghost,' she said to herself, and was pleased with the phrase. It made her feel as if somebody had given her a present."[8] A phrase told as a joke became a moment of transformation, a turning point in the life of that child of God.

Like that twelve-year-old girl, people all around us are waiting to overhear our witness. Such models of healing and transforming testimony continue when a boss tells a young coworker, "Excellent job!" or a teacher says to her students, "You are somebody." Thus, we hear anew the words of Peter in the New Testament when he wrote to new Christians, "You are a chosen people, a royal priesthood, a holy nation, God's special possession" (1 Peter 2:9). Are there not people all around us who need to hear such good words?

"If I have achieved anything in my life, it is because I have not been embarrassed to talk about God."

Dorothy Day

INVITED AND INVITING

Thomas Long, in his book *Testimony,* describes a moment of witness:

> A young bookstore clerk named Deborah arrived at work early to open the shop. Standing at the door waiting for the store to open was a man.... As Deborah was unlocking the door, the man quietly asked if he could come in. She hesitated; ... but the man seemed polite and evidently needed something right away, so she decided to let him come in early. After turning on the lights, she said, "Would you like any help?" Softly and with an accent he said, "Yes, I want to know about Jesus." This was not an altogether surprising request, since the store specialized in books on religion. So Deborah guided the man upstairs to the shop's ample section of books about Jesus.... "No," he said, "I want to know about Jesus the Messiah. Don't show me any more books. You tell me what you believe."[9]

AN INVITATION TO WITNESS

When we discover that we belong to Jesus Christ and to one another in the church, we have no option but to invite other people to that divine feast. Despite our hesitance, God can do marvelous things through our witness. As a bishop of the church once wrote:

> I invite you to share your story
> to give witness to ways in which God has fed you
> nurtured you
> led you
> and helped you to discern God's will.
> Try to keep it brief
> and honest.
> Permit God to guide you in the sharing.
> Allow God's spirit to speak to you
> and through you.
> To tell one's story is to build the reservoir of
> truth in the world.

Your experience is unlike that of any other person
and yet like every other person's.
Only you can share your part of the human
experience
only you can make this offering to God
only you can make this offering to the community
only you
only you.
And you will discover as others have discovered
that when you tell your story
the truth of it becomes plain
not only to the listener
but to you.[10]

---

1. From *The Lion, the Witch, and the Wardrobe: A Story for Children,* by C. S. Lewis (Macmillan, 1950); pages 18–19.

2. From *God Has A Story Too: Sermons in Context,* by James Saunders (Fortress, 1979); page v.

3. From www.seinfeldscripts.com/TheBurning.html.

4. Decimus Junius Juvenal.

5. From *Finding Faith,* by Sharon Gallagher (PageMill Press, 2001); pages 147–48.

6. From *Reaching Out: The Three Movements of the Spiritual Life,* by Henri J. M. Nouwen (Doubleday, 1975); page 51.

7. From "Hark! the Herald Angels Sing," by Charles Wesley, in *The United Methodist Hymnal* (Copyright © 1989 by The United Methodist Publishing House); 240.

8. From "A Temple of the Holy Ghost," in *The Complete Stories,* by Flannery O'Conner (Farrar, Straus & Girous, 1979); page 238.

9. From *Testimony: Talking Ourselves Into Being Christian,* by Thomas Long (Jossey-Bass, 2004); page 21.

10. Reuben Job in *Alive Now* (Upper Room, November/December 1988); pages 8–9.

What Next?

"It is not good for anyone to be alone."
Cheyenne Proverb

God has lighted the fire of Pentecost. The flames of baptism, Communion, prayer, miracles, stewardship, worship, hospitality, and witness continue to light our way and warm our lives. How will we stoke the fire and let it spread?

Some years ago, a series of tests was conducted at a public library regarding how to make the library experience more enjoyable for library patrons. In the first test, the librarians were instructed simply to hand the checked-out books over without any physical contact with the patrons. In the second test, librarians were instructed to touch the patrons on the hand when the book was delivered. The result was that twice as many patrons who were touched, as compared to patrons who were not touched, reported that they had had a pleasant experience at the library. Even subconsciously, everyone yearns to find a place to belong and to experience community. How will we assist in letting the flames of Pentecost shine so that the church continues to be a place of belonging?

"The virtuous soul that is alone . . . is like a lone burning coal. It will grow colder rather than hotter."
John of the Cross

CONTINUING TO BE IN COMMUNITY

Through the past ten weeks you have joined with other inquirers to ask some basic questions about how to live in community with other followers of Jesus Christ. In addition, you have learned how some Christians respond to those questions with regard to baptism, Holy Communion, prayer, signs and wonders, shared resources, worship, community, conflict resolution, and testimony. We pray that through these experiences you have found that you are not an island but a tree in the forest, with your roots entwined with many other trees. We hope that you have been caught up in the fiery passion of Pentecost.

Now is the time for you to consider how you will continue your spiritual journey. How will you risk finding community in your own life? What new behaviors will you adopt? Which old attitudes will you discard? Where will you go now that the study is over?

Begin by celebrating what you have already accomplished! Through your participation in the study you have demonstrated a steadfast effort to ask serious questions, engage in deep dialogue, and learn from other people who are also on a journey with God. You have begun to experience a part of the community called the church. On this journey, however, be aware that you may never arrive at a final destination. You and your group are making progress toward becoming the person and the loving community God created all of us to be.

We invite you to risk choosing to live a full, abundant, loving, and never-ending life with Jesus Christ in community with other people. Who does not wish to have such a life? Why would we choose to live a life that diminishes us, takes us down the wrong road, or leads us in the opposite direction from where we hope to be? Our society encourages us to be islands and live alone. Jesus Christ offers us the presence of God and other believers. Each of us has a choice. Now is the time for you to help create such a community where you live today.

"Be united with other Christians. A wall with loose bricks is not good. The bricks must be cemented together."

Corrie ten Boom

One important way to continue your growth in Jesus Christ is to remain connected with the people from your small group or class. You may have found some new friends and wish to continue those relationships. Your group may decide to remain together as a weekly Bible study group or Sunday school class. You might consider using the second study in the *Beginnings* series: *The Spiritual Life*. We anticipate that there will be a fourth study, *Sharing the New Creation*. We encourage you to sponsor a reunion of your small group a week or so after your class concludes for a supper or lunch meeting. See who comes, and make some plans together. The goal will be to encourage one another to grow together.

We especially urge you to consider bringing someone to the next session of *Beginnings: An Introduction to Christian Faith*. This first study in the *Beginnings* series introduces seekers and inquirers to the basic beliefs of Christianity by asking some questions: Who was Jesus Christ? What is the Bible? How do we pray? Why should we be a part of a community of believers?

Of course, the journey toward serious Christian discipleship is bigger than any study or series. We believe that active participation in the life of a Christian congregation is a critical part of the journey. The nurturing of your life in that community will take time and care, as you receive the ongoing guidance of the Spirit of God.

However you decide to continue your journey, please do so with intentionality, knowing that Jesus Christ through the Spirit is with you and your community in the journey toward wholeness. As basketball coach Mike Krzyzewski once wrote:

> You should live the journey.
> You should live it right.
> You should live it together.

You should live it shared.
You should try to make one another better.
You should get on one another if somebody's not doing their part.
You should hug one another when they are....
It's all about the journey....
Let's go.[1]

1. From LEADING WITH THE HEART, by MIKE KRZYZEWSKI. Copyright © 2000 by Mike Krzyzewski. Foreword © 2000 by Grant Hill. By permission of Grand Central Publishing.

Citations

ONE:
LONGING TO BELONG?
INTRODUCTION

Herbert Van Zeller quoted in *Checklist for Life for Women: Timeless Wisdom and Foolproof Strategies for Making the Most of Life's Challenges and Opportunities,* edited by Lila Empson (Thomas Nelson, 2002); page 61.

"Where Everybody Knows Your Name," by Judy Hart Angelo and Gary Portnoy (Addax Music Company).

John of the Cross quoted in *The Spirituality of Imperfection: Storytelling and the Search for Meaning,* by Ernest Kurtz and Katherine Ketchum (Bantam Books, 1992); page 89.

Mother Teresa quoted in *Sunbeams: A Book of Quotations,* edited by Sy Safransky (North Atlantic Books, 1990); page 29.

Desmond Tutu quoted in *Reconciliation: The Ubuntu Theology of Desmond Tutu,* by Michael Battle (The Pilgrim Press, 1997); page 35.

Hildegard of Bingen quoted in *Who Is Christ for Us?* by Dietrich Bonhoeffer (Fortress Press, 2002); page 67.

Bono quoted in *The Christian Century,* September 6, 2005; page 7.

"The Church," by Jason Vickers (unpublished paper, 2005); page 4.

Crossing the Unknown Sea: Work as a Pilgrimage of Identity, by David Whyte (Riverhead, 2001); page 23.

Life Together, by Dietrich Bonhoeffer (HarperCollins, 1954); page 20.

TWO:
HOW DO WE FIND OUR PLACE?
BAPTISM

William James quoted in *Sunbeams: A Book of Quotations,* edited by Sy Safransky (North Atlantic Books, 1990): page 5.

"Do You Wanna Dance"? © Bobby Freemon (ASCAP).

Latin Motto of the US.

© 1967 Fred M. Rogers (Family Comunications, Inc.).

J. Alec Motyer quoted in *Alive Now,* March/April 2005 (Upper Room, 2005); page 4.

The Fellowship of the Ring, by J.R.R. Tolkien (Houghton Mifflin, 1954); pages 115–16.

From "Why I Go to Church," by Tom Schaefer, in *The Charlotte Observer,* June 13, 2005; page 11A.

Traveling Mercies, by Anne Lamott (Pantheon, 1999); page 231.

Clement of Alexandria quoted in *Documents of Christian Worship,* by James C. White (John Knox, 1992); page 148. Edited for inclusive language.

"Counterscript: Living With the Elusive God," by Walter Brueggemann, in *The Christian Century,* November 29, 2005; page 26.

Christ Plays in Ten Thousand Places: A Conversation in Spiritual Theology, by Eugene Peterson (Eerdmans, 2005); page 304.

Christ Plays in Ten Thousand Places: A Conversation in Spiritual Theology, by Eugene Peterson; page 306.

THREE:
WHAT ARE WE HUNGRY FOR?
HOLY COMMUNION

"Hungry Heart," © Bruce Springsteen (ASCAP). © 2007 Sony BMG Music Entertainment, Inc.

From "You Satisfy the Hungry Heart" (Archdiocese of Philadelphia, 1977).

"Discovering Community," by Stephen V. Doughty, in *A Guide to Prayer for All Who Seek God,* by Reuben Job and Norman Shawchuck (Upper Room, 2003); pages 232–33.

"Broken and Shared," by Samuel Wells, in *The Christian Century,* June 14, 2005; page 8.

"Come, Sinners to the Gospel Feast," by Charles Wesley, in *The United Methodist Hymnal* (Copyright © 1989 by The United Methodist Publishing House, 1989); 616.

"Yours Are the Hands of Christ, by James Howell," in *A Guide to Prayer for All Who Seek God,* by Reuben Job and Norman Shawchuck; page 297.

"The Church, " by Hans Küng, in *A Guide to Prayer for Ministers and Other Servants,* by Reuben Job and Norman Shawchuck (Upper Room, 1983); page 56.

Mahatma Gandhi quoted in *Preaching the Movies,* by Edward McNulty (Geneva Press, 2001); page 153.

FOUR:
WHAT HAPPENS WHEN WE PRAY TOGETHER?
PRAYER

Reaching Out: The Three Movements of the Spiritual Life, by Henri J. M. Nouwen (Image Books, 1966); page 156.

The Golden String, by Bede Griffiths (P.J. Kennedy and Sons, 1955); page 130.

Christ Plays in Ten Thousand Places: A Conversation in Spiritual Theology, by Eugene Peterson (Eerdmans, 2005); page 279.

Rediscovering New Testament Prayer: Boldness and Blessing in the Name of Jesus, by John Koenig (HarperCollins, 1992); page 9.

Be Still and Know, by Michael Ramsey (Cowley, 1993); page 4.

Johanna Rogers Macy quoted in *Sunbeams: A Book of Quotations,* edited by Sy Safransky (North Atlantic Books, 1990); page 133.

The Body Broken: Answering God's Call to Love One Another, by Robert Benson (Doubleday, 2003); pages 124–25.

Morte D'Arthur, by Alfred, Lord Tennyson; line 415.

Life Together: A Discussion of Christian Fellowship, by Dietrich Bonhoeffer. Translated by John W. Doberstein (Harper and Row, 1954); page 86.

A Ray of Darkness: Sermons and Reflections, by Rowan Williams (Cowley, 1995); page 120.

FIVE: WHAT'S THE DEAL WITH MIRACLES? SIGNS AND WONDERS

Albert Einstein quoted in *Expect a Miracle: The Miraculous Things that Happen to Ordinary People,* by Dan Wakefield (Harper and Row, 1995); page 35.

Life After God, by Douglas Coupland (Pocket Books, 2002); page 51.

Life Is a Miracle: An Essay Against Modern Superstition, by Wendell Berry (Counterpoint, 2000); page 45.

Willa Cather quoted in *Expect a Miracle: The Miraculous Things That Happen to Ordinary People,* by Dan Wakefield; page 6.

Maurice Friedman quoted in *The Spirituality of Imperfection: Storytelling and the Search for Meaning,* by Ernest Kurtz and Katherine Ketchum (Bantam Books, 1992); page 118.

Acts: Brazos Theological Commentary on the Bible, by Jaroslav Pelikan (Brazos Press, 2005); page 98.

Willa Cather quoted in *Walking in This World: The Practical Art of Creativity*, by Julia Cameron (Jeremy P. Tarcher/Penguin, 2003); page 231.

The Death of Adam: Essays on Modern Thought, by Marilynne Robinson (Picador, 2005); page 243.

SIX: WHAT DO WE HAVE IN COMMON? STEWARDSHIP

Ignatius of Loyola quoted in *The Secrets of Jesuit Breadmaking,* by Brother Rick Curry (HarperPerennial, 1995); page 111.

Robert Frost quoted in *Sunbeams: A Book of Quotations,* edited by Sy Safransky (North Atlantic Books, 1990); page 11.

Myrtle Reed quoted in "Sunbeams," in *The Sun,* Issue 354, June 2004; page 48.

Greed, by Phyllis A. Tickle (Oxford University Press, 2004); pages 21–22.

Helen Walton in "Op Ed," in *The Charlotte Observer,* March 16, 2005; page P-1.

David Livingston quoted in *God and Your Stuff: The Vital Link Between Your Possessions and Your Soul,* by Wesley K. Willmer with Martyn Smith (NavPress, 2002); page 7.

The Book of Discipline of The United Methodist Church, 2004 (Copyright © 2004 by The United Methodist Publishing House); ¶103.

The Pilgrim's Progress, by John Bunyan, quoted in *Treasury of Religious Quotations,* edited by Gerald Tomlinson (Prentice Hall, 1991); page 93.

African Proverb quoted in "Op Ed," in *The Charlotte Observer,* March 16, 2005; page P-1.

Teresa of Avila quoted in *Yours Are the Hands of Christ: The Practice of Faith,* by James C. Howell (Upper Room, 1998); pages 9–10.

SEVEN: HOW CAN WE REMEMBER WHO WE ARE? WORSHIP

Dietrich Bonhoeffer quoted in *Finding Faith: Life-Changing Encounters With Christ,* by Sharon Gallagher (PageMill Press, 2001); page 51.

Pastor Kelly Clem in a conversation with Andy Langford.

Evelyn Underhill quoted in *Spiritual Classics,* by Richard Foster and Emilie Griffin (HarperSanFrancisco, 2000); page 254.

Dietrich Bonhoeffer in *Life Together,* quoted in *A Guide to Prayer for Ministers and Other Servants,* by Reuben Job and Norman Shawchuck (Upper Room, 1983); page 180.

Walter Brueggemann quoted in *Testimony,* by Thomas Long (Jossey-Bass, 2004); page xvii.

Harry Potter and the Goblet of Fire, by J. K. Rowling (Arthur A. Levine/Scholastic, 2000); page 712.

Doxology: The Praise of God in Worship, Doctrine, and Life, by Geoffrey Wainwright (Oxford University Press, 1980); page 422.

"Spiritual Life in the Congregation," by Reuben Job, in *A Guide to Prayer for All Who Seek God,* by Reuben Job and Norman Shawchuck (Upper Room, 2003); page 293.

"Electric Chimes or Ram's Horns," in *Grace Confounding,* by Amos Wilder (Fortress, 1972); page 13.

EIGHT:
HOW CAN WE OPEN OUR LIVES TO EACH OTHER?
HOSPITALITY

Mudhouse Sabbath, by Lauren Winner (Paraclete Press, 2003); page 47.
Reaching Out: The Three Movements of the Spiritual Life, by Henri J. M. Nouwen (Image Books, 1966); page 65.
Reaching Out: The Three Movements of the Spiritual Life, by Henri J. M. Nouwen. Quoted in *Christianity Today,* Vol. 49, No. 3, March 2005; page 74.
"Death of the Hired Man, " by Robert Frost, in *The Poetry of Robert Frost,* edited by Edward Connery Lathem (Henry Holt and Company, 1969); page 38.
Searching for Home: Spirituality for Restless Souls, by Craig Barnes (Brazos Press, 2003); page 67.
Augustine quoted in *Friendship and Society: An Introduction to Augustine's Practical Philosophy,* by Donald X. Burt (Eerdmans, 1999); page 57.
The Company of Strangers: Christians and the Renewal of America's Public Life, by Parker Palmer (Crossroad, 1981); page 67.
Sarah Jessica Parker as "Carrrie," in *Sex and the City* television series (© HBO).

NINE:
HOW CAN WE GET ALONG
WHEN WE ARE SO DIFFERENT?
CONFLICT RESOLUTION

Cool Hand Luke, screenplay by Donn Pearce (1967).
Beth Bussiere-Nichols quoted in *Plain Living: A Quaker Path to Simplicity,* by Catherine Whitmire (Sorin Books, 2001); page 144.
Parker Palmer quoted in *Plain Living: A Quaker Path to Simplicity,* edited by Catherine Whitmire; page 143.

New Seeds of Contemplation, by Thomas Merton (New Directions, 1961); page 72.

Church Conflict: From Contention to Collaboration, by Norma Cook Everist (Abingdon Press, 2004); page 155.

Kenneth Sutton quoted in *Plain Living: A Quaker Path to Simplicity,* edited by Catherine Whitmire; page 150.

The Life of the Beloved, by Henri J. M. Nouwen, quoted in *The Living Pulpit,* April/June 2004; page 41.

Muriel Bishop quoted in *Plain Living: A Quaker Path to Simplicity,* edited by Catherine Whitmire; page 146.

Leo Tolstoy quoted in *To See a World in a Grain of Sand,* by Caesar Johnson (Gibson, 1972); page 44.

An Autobiography: The Story of My Experiments With Truth, by Mohandas K. Gandhi (Beacon, 1957); pages 103, 437.

The Soul Would Have No Rainbow If the Eyes Had No Tears, by Guy Zona (Simon & Schuster, 1994); page 29.

Bono quoted in *The Christian Century,* September 6, 2005; page 7.

TEN:
HOW DO WE SHARE WHAT WE HAVE DISCOVERED?
WITNESS

"Venite Adoremus II," by D.T. Niles, in *World's Student Christian Federation Prayer Book*; pages 105ff.

Where God Happens: Discovering Christ in One Another, by Rowan Williams (New Seeds, 2005); page 27.

A Palpable God, by Reynolds Price (Atheneum, 1978); page 14.

Flip Wilson quoted on Virushead.net, "The First Collection."

"Out of the Saltshaker and Into the World," by Rebecca Manley Pippert, in *Fuel for the Journey,* by Lowell McNaney and Andy Lambert (Whitaker Ink, 2003); page 68.

Harold DeWolf quoted in *Faith Sharing,* by H. Eddie Fox and George E. Morris (Discipleship Resources, 1996); page 21.

Reuben Job in *A Guide to Prayer for All Who Seek God,* by Reuben Job and Norman Shawchuck (Upper Room, 2003); page 284.

Reuben Job in *A Guide to Prayer for All Who Seek God,* by Reuben Job and Norman Shawchuck; page 255

Dan Greene quoted in *Fuel for the Journey,* by Lowell McNaney and Andy Lambert (Whitaker Ink, 2003); page 69.

Peggy Way in *Alive Now,* November/December 1988 (Upper Room); page 4.

Testimony: Talking Ourselves Into Being Christian, by Thomas Long (Jossey-Bass, 2004); page 19.

William Temple quoted in *4400 Quotations for Christian Communicators,* by Carroll Simcox (Baker, 1991); page 68.

William Temple quoted in *Faith Sharing,* by H. Eddie Fox and George E. Morris; page 82.

Dorothy Day quoted in "A Biography of Dorothy Day," on Catholic Worker Home Page.

WHAT NEXT?

The Soul Would Have No Rainbow If the Eyes Had No Tears, by Guy Zona (Simon and Schuster, 1994); page 128.

John of the Cross quoted in *The Spirituality of Imperfection: Storytelling and the Search for Meaning,* by Ernest Kurtz and Katherine Ketchum (Bantam Books, 1992); page 89.

Corrie ten Boom quoted in *Fuel for the Journey,* by Lowell McNaney and Andy Lambert (Whitaker Ink, 2003); page 54

Notes